ARL ANNUAL SALARY SURVEY 2005-06

Compiled and Edited by

MARTHA KYRILLIDOU
MARK YOUNG

ASSOCIATION OF RESEARCH LIBRARIES
WASHINGTON, D.C.
2006

ARL Annual Salary Survey is published by

Association of Research Libraries
21 Dupont Circle, NW, Suite 800
Washington, D.C. 20036
Telephone: (202) 296-2296
FAX: (202) 872-0884
email: pubs@arl.org

Custom reports based on the *Salary Survey* data are also available. Contact the ARL Statistics and Measurement Program Officer for further information.

The quantitative rank order tables presented in this publication are not indicative of performance and outcomes and should not be used as measures of library quality. In comparing any individual library to ARL medians or to other ARL members, one must be careful to make such comparisons within the context of differing institutional and local goals and characteristics.

Visit the ARL Statistics and Measurement Program online at http://www.arl.org/stats/

ISSN 0361-5669
ISBN 1-59407-738-X

The paper used in this publication meets the minimum requirements of the American National Standard for Information Science and National Information Standards Organization standard—Permanence of Paper for Publications and Documents in Libraries and Archives, ANSI/NISO Z39.48-1992(R1997).

Printed in the United States of America

TABLE OF CONTENTS

U.S. ARL UNIVERSITY LIBRARIES

CANADIAN ARL UNIVERSITY LIBRARIES

ARL UNIVERSITY MEDICAL LIBRARIES

ARL UNIVERSITY LAW LIBRARIES

ARL ANNUAL SALARY SURVEY 2005-06

FOOTNOTES

APPENDIX A: ARL MEMBER LIBRARIES

APPENDIX B: TABLE NUMBERING CHANGES FOR 1998-99 to 1999-2000

SALARY SURVEY TRENDS 2005-06

The *ARL Annual Salary Survey 2005-06* reports salary data for all professional staff working in ARL libraries. The Association of Research Libraries (ARL) represents the interests of libraries that serve major North American research institutions. The Association operates as a forum for the exchange of ideas and as an agent for collective action to influence forces affecting the ability of these libraries to meet the future needs of scholarship. The ARL Statistics and Measurement program, which produces the *Salary Survey,* is organized around collecting, analyzing, and distributing quantifiable information describing the characteristics of research libraries. The *ARL Annual Salary Survey* is the most comprehensive and thorough guide to current salaries in large U.S. and Canadian academic and research libraries, and is a valuable management and research tool.

Data for 9,655 professional staff members were reported this year for the 113 ARL university libraries, including their law and medical libraries (913 staff members reported by 71 medical libraries and 746 staff members reported by 75 law libraries). For the 10 nonuniversity ARL members, data were reported for 3,921 professional staff members.

The tables are organized in seven major sections. The first section includes Tables 1 through 4, which report salary figures for all professionals working in ARL member libraries, including law and medical library data. The second section includes salary information for the 10 nonuniversity research libraries of ARL. The third section, entitled "ARL University Libraries," reports data in Tables 7 through 25 for the "general" library system of the university ARL members, combining U.S. and Canadian data but excluding law and medical data. The fourth section, composed of Tables 26 through 30, reports data on U.S. ARL university library members excluding law and medical data; the fifth section, Tables 31–34, reports data on Canadian ARL university libraries excluding law and medical data. The sixth section (Tables 35–41) and the seventh section (Tables 42–48) report on medical and law libraries, respectively, combining U.S. and Canadian data.

The university population is generally treated in three distinct groups: staff in the "general" library system, staff in the university medical libraries, and staff in the university law libraries. Any branch libraries for which data were received, other than law and medical, are included in the "general" category, whether or not those libraries are administratively independent. Footnotes for many institutions provide information on branch inclusion or exclusion.

In all tables where data from U.S. and Canadian institutions are combined, Canadian salaries are converted into U.S. dollar equivalents at the rate of 1.24971 Canadian dollars per U.S. dollar.[1] Tables 4 and 31 through 34, however, pertain exclusively to staff in Canadian university libraries, so salary data in those tables are expressed in Canadian dollars.

---

[1] This is the average monthly noon exchange rate published in the *Bank of Canada Review* for the period July 2004-June 2005 and is used in converting 2005-06 figures that are collected as of July 2005.

RACE AND ETHNICITY

There were 1,140 minority professional staff reported in 99 U.S. ARL university libraries, including law and medical.[2] Note that the data for minority professionals comes only from the U.S. ARL university libraries following the Equal Employment Opportunity Commission (EEOC) definitions; Canadian law prohibits the identification of Canadians by ethnic category.

Currently, 13.1% of the professional staff in U.S. ARL university libraries (including law and medical) belongs to one of the four non-Caucasian categories for which ARL keeps records. The number of minorities in managerial or administrative positions in the largest U.S. academic libraries is far lower: 5.1% are directors (5 out of 98), 6.9% are associate or assistant directors (26 out of 378), and 10% are branch librarians (46 out of 462). Graph 1, below, depicts the overall racial/ethnic distribution of professional staff in U.S. ARL university libraries: Caucasian/Other 86.9%, Asian/Pacific Islander 5.9%, Black 4.6%, Hispanic 2.4%, and American Indian/Alaskan Native 0.3%. According to a 1998 survey by Mary Jo Lynch, data from the American Library Association (ALA) show that the sample of academic libraries surveyed by ALA has a higher representation of Blacks, Asian/Pacific Islanders, and American Indian/Alaskan Native than ARL libraries.[3]

Graph 1
Ethnicity/Race of Professional Staff in
U.S. ARL University Libraries, 2005-06

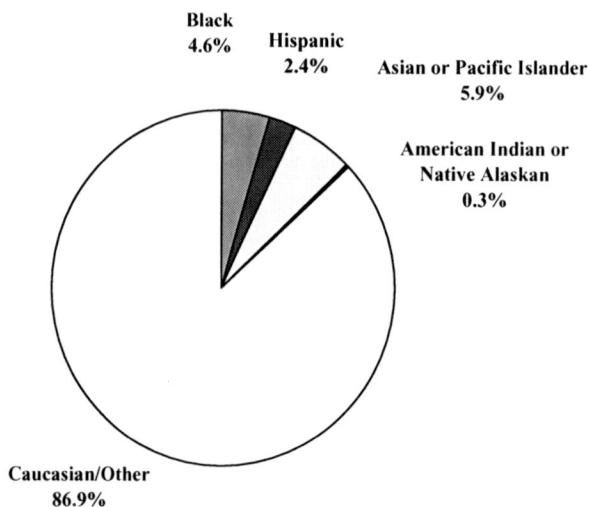

Black 4.6%   Hispanic 2.4%   Asian or Pacific Islander 5.9%

American Indian or Native Alaskan 0.3%

Caucasian/Other 86.9%

---

[2] Some U.S. institutions offer their librarians the option of not reporting race and ethnicity; others forbid the tracking of racial and ethnic classification altogether. See Footnotes.

[3] Mary Jo Lynch, "Librarians' Salaries: Smaller Increases This Year," *American Libraries* 29.10 (1998): 66-70. Also available at <http://www.ala.org/alaorg/ors/racethnc.html>.

Minority professional staff in U.S. ARL university libraries continues to be disproportionately distributed across the country. Using Figure 1, we can compare the number of minority staff with other staff, region by region. These patterns of distribution have been relatively stable for the entire history of ARL's data-collection experience. Minorities are underrepresented by more than 25% in the New England and West North Central regions (see Table 25 for a definition of the regions). Proportionately to other regions, there are more minorities in the South Atlantic, West South Central, and Pacific regions.

Figure 1

MINORITY PROFESSIONALS BY REGION (U.S.)
IN ARL UNIVERSITY LIBRARIES, FY 2005-06

	New England	Middle Atlantic	E North Central	W North Central	South Atlantic	East S Central	West S Central	Mountain	Pacific	TOTAL	%
Race/Ethnicity Category											
Black	32	60	82	24	110	21	21	10	38	398	35%
Hispanic	21	24	22	7	37	4	33	26	33	207	18%
Asian	66	81	76	21	66	8	39	24	130	511	45%
AI/AN[4]	3	3	4	3	5		2	4		24	2%
Minority Total	122	168	184	55	218	33	95	64	201	1,140	100%
Minority Percent	10.70%	14.74%	16.14%	4.82%	19.12%	2.89%	8.33%	5.61%	17.63%		
Nonminority Total	1,128	1,197	1,337	514	1,219	373	586	442	764	7,560	100%
Nonminority Percent	14.92%	15.83%	17.69%	6.80%	16.12%	4.93%	7.75%	5.85%	10.11%		
Regional Percent Total staff	14.37%	15.69%	17.48%	6.54%	16.52%	4.67%	7.83%	5.82%	11.09%		
Proportional Minority Representation	-28.28%	-6.93%	-8.74%	-29.04%	18.60%	-41.33%	7.51%	-3.98%	74.47%		

ARL recognizes the difficulties that the profession has in attracting a diverse workforce and continues to work actively in the development of workplace climates that embrace diversity. The ARL Diversity Program, through its Leadership and Career Development Program and the Initiative to Recruit a Diverse Workforce, emphasizes ARL and its members' commitment to creating a diverse academic and research library community to better meet the new challenges of global competition and changing demographics. Further, the Diversity Program focuses on issues surrounding work relationships in libraries while considering the impact of diversity on library services, interactions with library users, and the development of collections, at its homepage, http://www.arl.org/diversity/index.html.

Women comprise 70.53% of the four racial/ethnic groups that comprise minority staff, as compared to 62.99% of Caucasian/Other staff in all U.S. ARL university libraries. The overall

---

[4] American Indian/Alaskan Native.

gender balance in the 113 Canadian and U.S. university libraries (including law and medical) is 35.53% male and 64.47% female. See Figure 1, above, and Figure 2, below, for more detail on race/ethnic and gender distribution.

FIGURE 2
RACE/ETHNICITY AND SEX DISTRIBUTION OF PROFESSIONAL STAFF
IN ARL UNIVERSITY LIBRARIES FY 2005-06

United States					
	Men		Women		Total
	Number of Staff	Percent of Total	Number of Staff	Percent of Total	
Main	2,664	37.14%	4,508	62.86%	7,172
Medical	224	27.22%	599	72.78%	823
Law	246	34.89%	459	65.11%	705
Minority[5]	336	29.47%	804	70.53%	1,140
Non-minority	2,798	37.01%	4,762	62.99%	7,560
All	3,134	36.02%	5,566	63.98%	8,700
Canada					
	Men		Women		Total
	Number of Staff	Percent of Total	Number of Staff	Percent of Total	
Main	271	32.89%	553	67.11%	824
Medical	12	13.33%	78	86.67%	90
Law	13	31.71%	28	68.29%	41
All	296	30.99%	659	69.01%	
United States and Canada (Combined)					
	Men		Women		Total
	Number of Staff	Percent of Total	Number of Staff	Percent of Total	
Main	2,935	36.71%	5,061	63.29%	7,996
Medical	236	25.85%	677	74.15%	913
Law	259	34.72%	487	65.28%	746
All	3,430	35.53%	6,225	64.47%	

GENDER DATA

Many readers of previous surveys have inquired about evidence of gender-based salary differentials in ARL libraries. Data on salary comparisons for directors also are frequently requested. The average salary for male directors was higher than that of their female counterparts (see Table 17); however, the number of women in the top administrative library position has been growing steadily in recent years (63 women directors out of 112 total directorships reported).

Looking at other job categories, though, as Table 17 demonstrates, average salaries for men in most cases still surpass those of women in the same job category. In only 9 categories of the 27 used in the tables do the average salaries of women exceed those of men. The overall salary for women is 95.47% that of men for the 113 ARL university libraries, compared to 94.78% in 2004-05. This shows a marked closure of the gender gap in ARL libraries in the long term – in 1980-81, women in ARL libraries made roughly 87% that of men.

---

[5] Includes staff in medical and law libraries.

Table 18 provides average years of professional experience for many of the same staffing categories for which salary data are shown in Table 17, revealing that experience differentials between men and women cannot account fully for the salary differentials. Women average more experience in all but one of the categories in which they average higher pay, but there are other categories in which women on average have more experience and less pay (Assistant Director, Functional Specialist, and Subject Specialist are examples). Table 19 further reveals that the average salary for men is consistently higher than the average salary for women in all ten of the experience cohorts, a pattern that is also repeated for minority librarians: the average salary for minority men is higher than that for minority women in 8 out of 10 experience cohorts (see Table 30).

There is a sense that the gender gap persists in academe in areas beyond the library and that a renewed commitment to resolve the problem is needed.[6] A variety of reasons have been offered as to why these trends persist, most notably the perception that work is peripheral in a woman's life and, consequently, female-dominated professions are undervalued. Librarianship is predominantly and persistently a woman's profession. The scarcity of men in the profession has been well documented in many studies—the largest percentage of men employed in ARL libraries was 38.2% in 1980-81; since then men have consistently represented about 35% of the professional staff in ARL libraries.

THE FUNCTIONAL SPECIALIST BREAKDOWN

In 2004, the ARL Statistics and Measurement Committee accepted a proposal from the ACRL Personnel Administrators and Staff Development Officers Discussion Group to break down the Functional Specialist category. The Group's major concern was that so many different types of positions, with their varying job descriptions and salaries, were being labeled with the code FSPEC that data reported for the category were beginning to lose meaning. For each position that would have been labeled FSPEC in past years, the proposal offered ARL institutions two options: either use one of eight new codes to describe that position; or, if none of the eight new codes could adequately describe that position, use FSPEC. As seen in Figure 3a, almost one-fourth of Functional Specialists in all libraries did not use one of the alternative codes. Of the 1,358 positions that did use an alternate code, 54.1% of them were Archivists or Information Technology specialists.

---

[6] There are many instances citing the continuation of gender inequity in academia. See, for example: Denise K. Manger's articles in the *Chronicle of Higher Education*, "Faculty Salaries Increased 3.7% in 1999-2000" (14 Apr. 2000: A20) and "Faculty Salaries are Up 3.6%, Double the Rate of Inflation" (23 Apr. 1999: A16); D. W. Miller, "Salary Gap Between Male and Female Professors Grows Over the Years, Study Suggests," *Chronicle of Higher Education*, Today's News, 27 Apr. 2000, <http://chronicle.com/daily/2000/04/2000042702n.htm>; and Yolanda Moses, "Salaries in Academe: The Gender Gap Persists," *Chronicle of Higher Education* 12 Dec. 1997: A60.

FIGURE 3a
DISTRIBUTION OF JOB SUB-CODES FOR FUNCTIONAL SPECIALIST

Position	Main		Law		Medical		All	
	No.	Percent	No.	Percent	No.	Percent	No.	Percent
Archivist	307	18.2%	4	12.5%	8	10.1%	319	17.7%
Business Manager	102	6.0%	3	9.4%	10	12.7%	115	6.4%
Human Resources	82	4.9%	0		3	3.8%	85	4.7%
IT – Programming	326	19.3%	0		11	13.9%	337	18.7%
IT – Systems	106	6.3%	7	21.9%	6	7.6%	119	6.6%
IT – Web Development	192	11.4%	3	9.4%	5	6.3%	200	11.1%
Media/Multimedia	83	4.9%	2	6.3%	2	2.5%	87	4.8%
Preservation/Conservation	91	5.4%	2	6.3%	3	3.8%	96	5.3%
Other Functional Specialists	400	23.7%	11	34.4%	31	39.2%	442	24.6%
Total	**1,689**		**32**		**79**		**1,800**	

Figure 3b, below, displays the average salaries of the subcategories by position and sex, in the same fashion as Table 17. The salaries in each of the sub-categories deviate widely about the combined Functional Specialist average salary of $56,491. Human Resources specialists have the highest average of all subcategories, with an average salary of $63,896; specialists in Media/Multimedia have the lowest average salary of $48,924.

FIGURE 3b
DISTRIBUTION OF JOB SUB-CODES FOR FUNCTIONAL SPECIALIST

Position	Women		Men		Total	
	Salary	No.	Salary	No.	Salary	No.
Archivist	$53,753	186	$56,100	121	$54,678	307
Business Manager	59,140	67	65,399	35	61,288	102
Human Resources	62,906	72	71,029	10	63,896	82
IT – Programming	57,903	124	56,767	202	57,199	326
IT – Systems	57,675	52	54,827	54	56,224	106
IT – Web Development	60,746	62	61,321	130	61,135	192
Media/Multimedia	52,579	35	46,259	48	48,924	83
Preservation/Conservation	54,962	60	59,995	31	56,677	91
Other Functional Specialists	53,805	271	54,208	129	53,935	400
All Functional Specialists (See Table 17)	**$61,083**	**5,061**	**$63,984**	**2,935**	**$62,148**	**7,996**

In regards to the gender gap in ARL libraries explained in the previous section, it is worth noting that the average salaries of men are higher than those of women in six of the nine categories in Figure 3b.

INSTITUTIONAL CHARACTERISTICS AND SALARIES

A. PUBLIC AND PRIVATE INSTITUTIONS

The gap between salaries paid in private U.S. ARL university libraries and those paid in publicly supported U.S. university libraries widened in 2005-06 to 6.9%, or an average of $4,204 more paid for a position in a private institution. However, there were fewer categories than ever before in which average salaries in the public sector exceeded those paid for similar positions in private university libraries; only Heads of Serials, Circulation, Rare Books, and Reference Librarians with over 14 years of experience were paid more on average in public institutions (see Table 21).

B. LIBRARY SIZE

Library size, as measured by the number of professional staff, is another significant determinant of salary. As a rule, the largest libraries pay the highest average salaries, not only overall, but for specific positions as well. The cutoff staffing levels used to determine the largest cohort of libraries, after declining in every year since 1995-96, continued to hold steady at 110 in 2005-06.[7] The "largest" libraries, those with more than 110 staff members, reported the highest average salary, $65,878, compared to $62,974 for the cohort with between 75 and 110 staff. Libraries with between 22 and 49 professionals paid an average salary of $61,355 and those with staff between 50 and 74 paid $59,459. The gap between the highest paying cohort and the lowest paying cohort is $6,419, about 8.8% smaller than last year's difference of $7,041 (see Table 23).

C. GEOGRAPHIC AREA

The highest salaries are found in the Pacific region (see Table 25), followed by New England and the Middle Atlantic. All three areas have overall average salaries higher than $64,900, with the Pacific averaging as high as $68,789. The U.S./Canadian exchange rate has dropped precipitously over the past three years (see Table 4); as a result, Canada has shed its position as the region with the lowest average salary, which it had held since the early 1990s. Instead the West South Central region had the lowest average salary with an average of $55,267.

D. RANK STRUCTURE

Rank structure continues to provide a useful framework for examining professional salaries in ARL university libraries. Figure 4, below, displays average salary and years of experience in the most commonly used rank structures. Readers should be aware that not all individuals have a rank that fits into the rank structure the library utilizes. Most commonly, directors may have no rank or a rank outside the structure, and it is common for non-librarians included in the survey (business officers, personnel staff, computer specialists, etc.) to be unranked, as well.

---

[7] In 1995-96, the largest cohort of libraries was determined based on staff over 124; in 1996-98, over 120; in 1998-99, over 115; and since 1999-2000, over 110. See Table 23.

The pattern of relationships between rank and salary seen in past years continues, where higher rank is associated with higher average years of experience and a higher salary. 6,048 of the 9,655 librarians in ARL university member libraries occupy a rank within these three most commonly found ranking systems, and the largest number of professionals (3,349) occupies a rank in a four-step rank structure.

Figure 4

**AVERAGE SALARIES AND AVERAGE YEARS OF EXPERIENCE OF LIBRARY PROFESSIONALS
IN LIBRARIES WITH THREE, FOUR, AND FIVE STEP RANK STRUCTURES
FY 2005-06**

	Three-Step		Four-Step		Five-Step	
	Salary	Experience	Salary	Experience	Salary	Experience
Librarian 1	$46,740	7.4	$46,073	8.4	$45,509	9.0
Librarian 2	57,795	17.4	50,902	11.8	53,954	12.3
Librarian 3	75,831	25.2	61,982	19.8	61,259	19.2
Librarian 4			75,283	25.4	74,349	23.6
Librarian 5					89,628	28.5
No. of Staff	1,363		3,349		1,336	

INFLATION EFFECT

Tables 2 and 6 reveal changes in beginning professional and median salaries, as well as changes in the U.S. Bureau of Labor's Cost of Living Index (CPI-U) for university and nonuniversity research libraries. Table 3 is similar to Table 2, but reports data only on U.S. libraries. Table 4 shows trend data for Canadian libraries and compares them to the Canadian Consumer Price Index changes. Tables 2, 3, and 4 include law and medical library staff in ARL university libraries. All tables indicate that the purchasing power of professionals working in ARL libraries is keeping up with inflation.

The median salary for all ARL university libraries was $57,074 in 2005-06; for only U.S. ARL libraries it was $57,173; and for Canadian ARL libraries converted into U.S. dollars it was $56,474, or a median of $70,576 Canadian dollars.

Table 6 reveals that the median salary for nonuniversity staff has increased about 2.8% in the last year. The median salary for combined U.S. and Canadian university libraries increased 3.3% (Table 2); U.S. salaries alone increased 2.8% (Table 3). Although Canadian salaries in U.S. dollars increased sharply due to changes in the currency exchange rate, Canadian salaries denominated in Canadian dollars actually dropped 0.3% (Table 4). At the same time, the U.S. Consumer Price Index increased 3.2% in the last year and the Canadian Consumer Price Index increased 2.0%.

Beginning salaries in the university sector continue to increase at a steady rate. The median beginning salary in ARL university libraries increased to $37,920; this 2.5% increase is slightly less than the increase reported in 2004-05. After three consecutive years of increasing by 1% or less, the median beginning salary for ARL nonuniversity research libraries jumped by 11.2% to $38,673.

Libraries are facing serious human resources issues as the need to hire professionals with advanced technological skills and the demand for these skills pushes salaries up while libraries seem unable to adjust their salary structures beyond accounting for inflation. As people are hired with higher beginning salaries, the inability to adjust the overall salary structure to achieve some equity for the experienced staff members is another factor that contributes to slow salary growth. This, combined with other evidence from the *ARL Statistics,* shows libraries' proportion of materials and operating expenditures increasing faster than salaries, providing a future picture of libraries with fewer staff members, who are in turn being paid salaries that are fighting to keep up with inflation.

Readers are reminded that these data reflect only salaries, and that there are other compensation issues, which may have influenced the pattern of salaries in various institutions. In addition, a highly standardized structure for capturing data has been used, which may portray results in a way that cannot be fully representative of a local situation.

Martha Kyrillidou
Mark Young
Association of Research Libraries
May 1, 2006

SALARY LEVELS FOR STAFF IN ARL LIBRARIES

Tables 1–4

TABLE 1: DISTRIBUTION BY SALARY LEVEL*

Figures in columns headed by fiscal year show the number of filled professional positions. Columns headed by cum. % show the percentage of all filled positions with salaries equal to or more than the beginning of each salary range. For example, in FY 2005-06, 68.9% of all ARL university librarians earned more than $50,000, as did 87.6% of all ARL nonuniversity librarians.

Salary Range	University Librarians				Nonuniversity Librarians			
	FY 2004-05	cum. %	FY 2005-06	cum. %	FY 2004-05	cum. %	FY 2005-06	Cum. %
More than 250,000	5	0.1%	9	0.1%	0	0.0%	1	0.0%
200,000 - 250,000	16	0.2%	21	0.3%	0	0.0%	0	0.0%
175,000 - 199,999	31	0.5%	29	0.6%	1	0.0%	1	0.1%
150,000 - 174,999	52	1.1%	60	1.2%	5	0.2%	7	0.2%
140,000 - 149,999	28	1.4%	39	1.6%	98	2.6%	102	2.8%
130,000 - 139,999	37	1.8%	45	2.1%	170	6.9%	190	7.7%
120,000 - 129,999	54	2.4%	45	2.6%	106	9.6%	110	10.5%
110,000 - 119,999	75	3.1%	103	3.6%	189	14.4%	222	16.1%
100,000 - 109,999	152	4.7%	186	5.6%	187	19.2%	247	22.4%
95,000 - 99,999	114	5.9%	127	6.9%	125	22.3%	165	26.7%
90,000 - 94,999	142	7.4%	183	8.8%	225	28.0%	190	31.5%
85,000 - 89,999	243	10.0%	244	11.3%	226	33.8%	251	37.9%
80,000 - 84,999	288	13.0%	381	15.2%	221	39.4%	343	46.6%
76,000 - 79,999	303	16.2%	347	18.8%	357	48.4%	213	52.1%
74,000 - 75,999	167	18.0%	209	21.0%	106	51.1%	136	55.5%
72,000 - 73,999	194	20.0%	229	23.4%	151	54.9%	72	57.4%
70,000 - 71,999	259	22.8%	287	26.3%	71	56.7%	76	59.3%
68,000 - 69,999	241	25.3%	253	29.0%	73	58.6%	183	64.0%
66,000 - 67,999	291	28.4%	304	32.1%	98	61.0%	81	66.1%
64,000 - 65,999	352	32.1%	361	35.9%	186	65.8%	136	69.5%
62,000 - 63,999	351	35.8%	343	39.4%	105	68.4%	120	72.6%
60,000 - 61,999	375	39.7%	413	43.7%	155	72.4%	37	73.5%
58,000 - 59,999	359	43.5%	401	47.8%	49	73.6%	99	76.1%
56,000 - 57,999	443	48.2%	494	53.0%	82	75.7%	110	78.9%
54,000 - 55,999	481	53.3%	478	57.9%	75	77.6%	144	82.5%
52,000 - 53,999	510	58.6%	526	63.4%	139	81.1%	153	86.4%
50,000 - 51,999	525	64.2%	538	68.9%	184	85.8%	44	87.6%
48,000 - 49,999	542	69.9%	511	74.2%	77	87.7%	109	90.3%
46,000 - 47,999	533	75.5%	505	79.5%	87	89.9%	68	92.1%
44,000 - 45,999	479	80.6%	510	84.7%	63	91.5%	134	95.5%
42,000 - 43,999	488	85.7%	448	89.4%	130	94.8%	95	97.9%
40,000 - 41,999	411	90.0%	387	93.4%	90	97.1%	29	98.6%
38,000 - 39,999	309	93.3%	231	95.8%	40	98.1%	18	99.1%
36,000 - 37,999	273	96.2%	191	97.8%	34	99.0%	15	99.5%
34,000 - 35,999	204	98.3%	122	99.0%	26	99.6%	12	99.8%
32,000 - 33,999	96	99.3%	56	99.6%	8	99.8%	3	99.9%
30,000 - 31,999	40	99.7%	20	99.8%	4	99.9%	1	99.9%
less than 30,000	24	100.0%	19	100.0%	3	100.0%	4	100.0%
Total Positions	**9,487**		**9,655**		**3,946**		**3,921**	
Median Salary	**$55,250**		**$57,074**		**$74,022**		**$76,083**	

* Canadian salaries expressed in U.S. dollars. Includes medical and law libraries.

TABLE 2: SALARY TRENDS IN ARL UNIVERSITY LIBRARIES*

Salary figures for the current year are displayed in the context of the previous years and compared to the changes in the Consumer Price Index (CPI) to show trends in the purchasing power of median and beginning professional salaries. Salary figures and CPI numbers have been converted to adjusted indexes using July 1984 as the base. Actual CPI data retrieved from the U.S. Department of Labor, Bureau of Labor Statistics' *Consumer Price Index for All Urban Consumers - (CPI-U)*, located at http://146.142.4.24/cgi-bin/surveymost?cu.

Fiscal Year	No. of Libs.	Total Staff	Median Salary†	BPS‡ Median	Median Salary Index	BPS‡ Index	Actual CPI	Adjusted CPI
2005-06	113	9,655	$57,074	$37,920	218.7	229.8	195.4	188.1
2004-05	113	9,487	55,250	36,984	211.7	224.1	189.4	182.3
2003-04	114	9,492	53,000	36,000	203.1	218.2	183.9	177.0
2002-03	114	9,469	51,636	35,000	197.8	212.1	180.1	173.3
2001-02	113	9,198	50,724	34,000	194.3	206.1	177.5	170.8
2000-01	112	8,882	49,068	32,879	188.0	199.3	172.8	166.3
1999-2000	111	8,595	47,377	31,100	181.5	188.5	166.7	160.4
1998-99	110	8,400	45,775	30,000	175.2	181.7	163.2	157.1
1997-98	110	8,414	44,534	28,500	170.5	172.6	160.5	154.5
1996-97	109	8,325	43,170	27,687	165.3	167.7	157.0	151.1
1995-96	108	8,231	41,901	27,000	160.5	163.6	152.5	146.8
1994-95	108	8,216	41,088	26,000	157.4	157.6	148.4	142.8
1993-94	108	8,132	40,225	25,834	154.1	156.6	144.4	139.0
1992-93	108	8,212	39,265	25,000	150.4	151.5	140.2	134.9
1991-92	107	8,256	38,537	24,000	147.7	145.5	136.2	131.1
1990-91	107	8,382	36,701	23,800	140.6	144.2	130.7	125.8
1989-90	107	8,253	34,629	22,000	132.7	133.3	124.0	119.3
1988-89	107	8,087	32,461	20,400	124.4	123.6	118.3	113.9
1987-88	106	7,962	30,534	19,460	117.0	117.9	113.6	109.3
1986-87	105	7,718	28,941	18,250	110.9	110.6	109.6	105.5
1985-86	105	7,543	27,485	17,500	105.3	106.1	107.6	103.6
1984-85	104	7,161	26,100	16,500	100.0	100.0	103.9	100.0

* Canadian salaries expressed in U.S. dollars.
† Includes medical and law libraries.
‡ Beginning professional salary.

TABLE 3: SALARY TRENDS IN U.S. ARL UNIVERSITY LIBRARIES*

Salary figures for the current year are displayed in the context of previous years and compared to the changes in the U.S. Consumer Price Index (CPI) to show trends in the purchasing power of median and beginning professional salaries. Salary figures and CPI numbers have been converted to adjusted indexes, using July 1984 as the base. Actual CPI data retrieved from the U.S. Department of Labor, Bureau of Labor Statistics' *Consumer Price Index for All Urban Consumers - (CPI-U)*, located at http://146.142.4.24/cgi-bin/surveymost?cu.

Fiscal Year	No. of Libs.	Total Staff	Median Salary	Median Salary Change	Median Salary Index	Actual CPI	Adjusted CPI	CPI Change
2005-06	99	8,700	$57,173	2.8%	220.4	195.4	188.1	3.2%
2004-05	99	8,581	55,600	3.2	214.3	189.4	182.3	3.0
2003-04	100	8,581	53,859	2.0	207.6	183.9	177.0	2.1
2002-03	100	8,544	52,789	1.9	203.5	180.1	173.3	1.5
2001-02	99	8,337	51,806	4.1	199.7	177.5	170.8	2.7
2000-01	99	8,127	49,753	3.7	191.8	172.8	166.3	3.7
1999-2000	98	7,858	48,000	4.1	185.0	166.7	160.4	2.1
1998-99	97	7,671	46,130	3.6	177.8	163.2	157.1	1.7
1997-98	97	7,682	44,544	3.4	171.7	160.5	154.5	2.2
1996-97	96	7,562	43,084	3.4	166.1	157.0	151.1	3.0
1995-96	95	7,435	41,651	2.7	160.5	152.5	146.8	2.8
1994-95	95	7,401	40,573	3.4	156.4	148.4	142.8	2.8
1993-94	95	7,390	39,257	3.0	151.3	144.4	139.0	3.0
1992-93	95	7,375	38,124	3.0	146.9	140.2	134.9	2.9
1991-92	94	7,408	37,009	3.5	142.6	136.2	131.1	4.2
1990-91	94	7,543	35,761	5.2	137.8	130.7	125.8	5.4
1989-90	94	7,344	34,000	5.8	131.0	124.0	119.3	4.8
1988-89	94	7,252	32,149	5.4	123.9	118.3	113.9	4.1
1987-88	93	7,145	30,492	5.1	117.5	113.6	109.3	3.6
1986-87	92	6,886	29,021	6.5	111.9	109.6	105.5	1.9
1985-86	91	6,707	27,249	5.0	105.0	107.6	103.6	3.6
1984-85	91	6,456	25,946	6.9	100.0	103.9	100.0	-

* Includes medical and law libraries in median salary.

TABLE 4: SALARY TRENDS IN CANADIAN ARL UNIVERSITY LIBRARIES*

Salary figures for the current year are displayed in the context of previous years. Canadian salaries are presented in both U.S. $ and Canadian $ denominations and the annual exchange rate used in the salary surveys is also listed. Canadian salaries are also compared to the changes in the Canadian Consumer Price Index (CPI) to show trends in the purchasing power of median Canadian salaries. CPI number changes are based on July CPI figures. The Canadian CPI change is indicated in the DATE edition of *The Daily*, a Statistics Canada publication, at http://www.statcan.ca/english/Subjects/Cpi/cpi-en.htm.

Fiscal Year	No. of Libs.	Total Staff	Median Salary in U.S. $†	Median Salary Change†	Exchange Rate	Median Salary in Can. $	Median Salary Change	Canadian CPI Change
2005-06	14	955	$56,474	7.1%	1.24971	$70,576	-0.3%	2.0%
2004-05	14	906	52,707	16.3	1.34328	70,800	3.5	2.3
2003-04	14	911	45,310	6.2	1.51023	68,429	2.3	2.2
2002-03	14	925	42,657	-0.6	1.56878	66,919	2.6	2.1
2001-02	14	861	42,928	-1.1	1.51919	65,215	2.1	2.6
2000-01	13	755	43,394	5.0	1.47192	63,873	2.4	3.0
1999-2000	13	737	41,316	-3.8	1.5103	62,400	2.4	1.8
1998-99	13	729	42,963	-2.7	1.4177	60,909	0.9	1.0
1997-98	13	732	44,167	1.4	1.3663	60,346	1.7	1.8
1996-97	13	764	43,569	0.9	1.3613	59,310	-0.4	1.2
1995-96	13	796	43,173	-1.7	1.3794	59,554	1.3	2.5
1994-95	13	815	43,919	-6.0	1.3381	58,768	0.7	0.2
1993-94	13	816	46,744	-4.3	1.2488	58,374	2.9	1.6
1992-93	13	837	48,820	2.7	1.1623	56,744	3.4	1.3
1991-92	13	847	47,519	5.5	1.1547	54,870	3.6	5.8
1990-91	13	839	45,023	15.1	1.1759	52,942	12.5	4.2
1989-90	13	853	39,117	12.3	1.2026	47,042	5.3	5.4
1988-89	13	837	34,826	11.7	1.2826	44,668	5.3	3.8
1987-88	13	817	31,178	10.9	1.3602	42,408	9.1	4.7
1986-87	13	831	28,123	-1.9	1.3817	38,858	1.2	4.2
1985-86	13	829	28,666	1.1	1.3388	38,378	7.9	3.8
1984-85	12	705	28,346	-0.8	1.2548	35,569	0.8	4.2
Average				2.5%			3.4%	

* Canadian salaries expressed in U.S. dollars.
† Includes medical and law libraries in median salary.

ARL NONUNIVERSITY LIBRARIES

Tables 5–6

TABLE 5: MEDIAN AND BEGINNING PROFESSIONAL SALARIES
IN ARL NONUNIVERSITY LIBRARIES*

		Median Salaries		Beginning Salaries	
	No. of Staff	FY 2004-05	FY 2005-06	FY 2004-05	FY 2005-06
Boston Public Library	183	$50,841	$54,217	$34,298	$37,491
Canada Institute for Scientific and Technical Information *	191	49,840	54,389	34,663	37,258
Center for Research Libraries	27	44,580	46,675	30,305	26,518
Library of Congress †	2,706	79,319	82,259	41,815	43,365
National Agricultural Library †	109	68,722	71,269	41,815	43,365
Library & Archives of Canada *	148	42,330	53,704	33,817	39,011
National Library of Medicine	185	74,785	79,652	41,815	43,365
New York Public Library	247	52,434	54,777	34,866	35,912
New York State Library	62	53,512	57,862	34,549	38,334
Smithsonian Library	63	69,732	71,269	41,815	43,365

* Canadian salaries expressed in U.S. dollars.
† See footnotes.

TABLE 6: SALARY TRENDS IN ARL NONUNIVERSITY LIBRARIES*

Salary figures for the current year are displayed in the context of the previous years and compared to the changes in the Consumer Price Index (CPI) to show trends in the purchasing power of median and beginning professional salaries. Salary figures and CPI numbers have been converted to adjusted indexes, using July 1984 as the base. Actual CPI data retrieved from the U.S. Department of Labor, Bureau of Labor Statistics' *Consumer Price Index for All Urban Consumers - (CPI-U)*, located at <http://146.142.4.24/cgi-bin/surveymost?cu>.

Fiscal Year	No. of Libs.	Total Staff	Median Salary*	BPS† Median	Median Salary Index	BPS† Index	Actual CPI	Adjusted CPI
2005-06	10	3,921	$76,083	$38,673	224.6	234.3	195.4	188.1
2004-05	10	3,946	74,022	34,764	218.5	210.6	189.4	182.3
2003-04	10	3,877	70,020	34,739	206.8	210.4	183.9	177.0
2002-03	10	3,804	65,289	34,739	192.7	210.4	180.1	173.3
2001-02	10	3,717	65,025	34,389	191.9	208.3	177.5	170.8
2000-01	10	3,731	62,521	31,774	184.5	192.5	172.8	166.3
1999-2000	10	3,737	59,916	30,849	176.8	186.9	166.7	160.4
1998-99	11	3,819	56,000	29,877	165.3	181.0	163.2	157.1
1997-98	11	3,779	55,055	28,724	162.5	174.0	160.5	154.5
1996-97	11	3,799	51,150	28,380	151.0	172.0	157.0	151.1
1995-96	11	3,915	49,149	28,162	145.1	170.7	152.5	146.8
1994-95	11	3,837	47,997	27,813	141.7	168.6	148.4	142.8
1993-94	11	4,003	44,949	26,806	132.7	162.5	144.4	139.0
1992-93	11	4,172	43,876	23,500	129.6	142.4	140.2	134.9
1991-92	11	2,906	42,455	23,500	125.4	142.4	136.2	131.1
1990-91	12	1,363	36,013	20,800	106.3	126.1	130.7	125.8
1989-90	11	3,767	40,106	20,195	118.4	122.4	124.0	119.3
1988-89	11	3,781	37,544	19,100	110.9	115.8	118.3	113.9
1987-88	11	3,765	36,250	18,405	107.0	111.5	113.6	109.3
1986-87	10	2,790	33,020	17,912	97.5	108.6	109.6	105.5
1985-86	12	3,874	33,720	17,308	99.6	104.9	107.6	103.6
1984-85	11	3,840	33,863	16,500	100.0	100.0	103.9	100.0

* Canadian salaries expressed in U.S. dollars.
† Beginning professional salary.

ARL UNIVERSITY LIBRARIES

Tables 7–25

TABLE 7: FILLED POSITIONS; AVERAGE, MEDIAN, BEGINNING PROFESSIONAL SALARIES; AND AVERAGE YEARS OF EXPERIENCE
ARL UNIVERSITY LIBRARIES, FY 2005-06*

Institution	Filled Pos. FY 2006	Average Salaries FY 2005	Average Salaries FY 2006	Median Salaries FY 2005	Median Salaries FY 2006	Beginning Salaries FY 2005	Beginning Salaries FY 2006	Average Yrs. Exp. FY 2006
Alabama ‡	49	$45,900	$52,161	$42,145	$48,114	$35,000	$35,000	14.7
Alberta †‡	65	58,593	63,237	61,316	67,656	32,689	36,366	16.9
Arizona	65	58,848	61,122	52,181	54,053	43,118	41,688	16.7
Arizona State ‡	69	53,217	56,240	51,628	54,866	38,000	38,000	17.5
Auburn ‡	47	53,850	56,868	50,865	55,175	40,930	42,570	15.8
Boston University	57	50,242	52,555	46,800	48,900	32,000	33,000	17.2
Boston College ‡	61	60,321	62,260	56,750	58,625	37,550	38,700	18.2
Brigham Young	105	57,637	59,699	55,390	57,500	42,300	43,100	18.2
British Columbia †‡	76	55,038	57,426	53,663	55,141	33,277	35,768	16.1
Brown ‡	65	60,107	61,624	58,069	58,573	34,650	35,500	21.2
California, Berkeley ‡	99	72,651	74,847	70,500	75,480	37,920	37,920	18.8
California, Davis ‡	42	68,339	69,263	70,500	70,500	37,920	37,920	19.4
California, Irvine	49	68,236	67,817	69,365	70,500	37,920	37,920	16.7
California, Los Angeles	139	72,036	72,477	71,592	70,500	37,920	37,920	18.1
California, Riverside ‡	39	64,091	63,730	64,164	61,724	37,920	40,560	17.2
California, San Diego ‡	75	67,498	68,199	65,000	65,000	37,920	37,920	16.5
California, Santa Barbara ‡	58	67,563	67,798	67,592	64,164	37,920	37,920	18.1
Case Western Reserve	34	53,387	55,194	50,293	53,500	35,000	35,000	13.6
Chicago	66	66,642	67,795	61,082	63,318	42,650	43,930	17.4
Cincinnati ‡	58	58,623	61,054	55,128	57,929	33,000	35,000	20.1
Colorado ‡	45	57,212	59,006	55,362	56,837	38,000	40,000	17.9
Colorado State ‡	44	59,003	59,725	57,650	56,150	39,000	39,000	16.9
Columbia	111	65,991	66,788	58,500	59,530	45,700	47,500	17.1
Connecticut ‡	54	68,254	71,115	62,981	66,666	45,000	48,000	16.6
Cornell ‡	117	61,673	64,443	55,000	57,768	40,000	41,600	17.0
Dartmouth ‡	48	64,221	66,275	63,521	63,704	28,119	37,000	16.3
Delaware ‡	57	62,936	65,175	61,007	63,314	39,000	39,000	17.2
Duke ‡	106	58,328	58,326	54,050	54,400	36,850	36,850	16.6
Emory ‡	73	58,976	60,657	56,100	57,525	35,000	37,000	14.7
Florida ‡	71	49,742	55,378	45,971	50,282	40,000	42,000	20.4
Florida State ‡	51	45,588	48,890	41,128	44,853	36,000	38,000	16.1
George Washington ‡	34	61,687	61,800	58,650	58,650	38,000	42,000	15.5
Georgetown ‡	49	61,195	62,118	57,214	58,017	40,000	42,000	19.6
Georgia ‡	68	50,847	52,547	47,278	48,023	32,000	32,000	17.0
Georgia Tech	35	55,274	57,097	55,080	51,497	40,000	44,000	14.4
Guelph †‡	39	50,616	57,165	48,596	55,570	30,662	33,781	18.6
Harvard ‡	452	64,912	67,247	59,845	61,987	42,100	43,600	16.1
Hawaii	56	57,357	59,748	55,872	58,068	36,727	36,720	17.3
Houston ‡	69	49,319	47,115	43,490	42,363	36,000	37,000	11.9
Howard	32	48,931	51,033	45,828	48,956	35,049	35,049	25.8
Illinois, Chicago ‡	56	57,712	57,470	51,693	51,764	36,000	42,000	16.1
Illinois, Urbana	140	58,423	60,878	52,265	54,213	42,000	42,000	13.7
Indiana ‡	82	60,025	59,557	57,281	56,000	35,869	36,227	18.6
Iowa	66	54,776	58,742	50,939	53,001	35,000	40,000	17.6
Iowa State ‡	54	54,419	56,262	53,114	54,751	38,000	40,000	18.1
Johns Hopkins	74	59,759	61,259	55,000	57,355	42,476	43,113	14.6
Kansas ‡	71	56,913	59,314	52,135	55,244	35,000	40,000	18.0
Kent State ‡	60	54,216	50,491	51,758	49,470	42,778	48,889	15.4
Kentucky ‡	66	50,800	54,086	47,864	52,785	36,000	37,500	18.5
Laval †	63	48,698	50,058	51,828	54,639	31,775	34,154	17.6
Louisiana State	52	44,141	43,882	41,444	40,188	35,000	35,800	13.1
Louisville ‡	37	57,383	60,837	55,908	61,114	35,000	36,000	21.4
McGill †‡	55	52,073	56,669	54,653	58,588	30,522	32,808	19.6
McMaster †‡	25	51,882	55,735	50,764	55,520	29,488	32,646	18.5
Manitoba †‡	43	57,169	63,923	59,837	66,036	31,688	35,083	22.9
Maryland ‡	100	57,943	59,218	55,083	55,848	40,000	40,000	17.7
Massachusetts ‡	49	65,949	65,120	66,437	65,640	37,274	37,274	17.9

*Directors are included in figures for average years of experience and filled positions, but not in either the average or median salary statistics. Excludes medical and law libraries. See Tables 35 and 42 for statistics related to medical and law library salaries.

† Canadian salaries expressed in U.S. dollars.

‡ See Footnotes.

TABLE 7: FILLED POSITIONS; AVERAGE, MEDIAN, BEGINNING PROFESSIONAL SALARIES; AND AVERAGE YEARS OF EXPERIENCE
ARL UNIVERSITY LIBRARIES, FY 2005-06*

Institution	Filled Pos. FY 2006	Average Salaries FY 2005	Average Salaries FY 2006	Median Salaries FY 2005	Median Salaries FY 2006	Beginning Salaries FY 2005	Beginning Salaries FY 2006	Average Yrs. Exp. FY 2006
MIT ‡	92	$63,513	$65,006	$58,200	$62,100	$43,800	$44,000	15.3
Miami ‡	37	55,431	59,425	53,233	55,349	36,000	38,000	21.3
Michigan ‡	108	58,856	63,448	53,349	57,527	35,000	40,000	18.4
Michigan State	64	59,803	60,069	56,750	57,800	41,000	43,000	17.2
Minnesota	109	56,176	62,872	53,603	59,776	36,000	36,000	19.1
Missouri ‡	37	52,059	51,922	46,431	47,559	32,000	32,500	20.9
Montreal ‡	90	47,396	50,998	47,060	50,583	29,971	33,241	16.1
Nebraska ‡	49	54,905	56,297	50,402	49,357	40,000	40,500	16.0
New Mexico ‡	38	65,770	68,175	66,226	66,598	39,900	40,000	20.9
New York	51	66,510	69,214	59,782	61,765	45,000	47,000	18.7
North Carolina	96	56,872	59,769	52,750	55,650	37,500	40,000	18.9
North Carolina State ‡	87	57,932	60,293	52,852	54,174	40,000	45,000	10.8
Northwestern ‡	83	59,657	61,459	57,493	58,397	34,000	36,000	17.6
Notre Dame ‡	51	61,008	61,908	59,281	59,380	36,000	36,000	18.8
Ohio University ‡	48	48,881	48,769	43,113	43,864	33,000	33,000	12.8
Ohio State ‡	103	56,375	57,760	52,277	54,911	39,500	40,000	19.7
Oklahoma	46	45,724	50,372	41,644	47,210	39,000	40,000	13.9
Oklahoma State ‡	50	43,972	51,414	40,236	47,376	34,000	34,000	16.0
Oregon	45	52,516	54,627	49,607	50,980	34,000	35,000	16.4
Pennsylvania ‡	82	58,659	60,456	55,575	57,233	40,000	40,000	17.4
Pennsylvania State ‡	132	61,145	62,619	57,912	59,436	38,500	39,000	17.9
Pittsburgh ‡	63	55,963	59,357	50,324	55,414	30,000	30,000	16.4
Princeton ‡	103	68,399	71,845	62,700	67,300	40,000	40,000	21.3
Purdue ‡	57	57,050	60,839	50,600	55,535	36,500	42,000	18.0
Queen's †‡	34	54,936	61,355	54,609	61,342	31,378	34,738	19.3
Rice ‡	56	55,150	57,524	49,113	51,100	34,527	34,527	15.5
Rochester ‡	67	47,775	51,184	45,557	48,339	36,000	36,000	15.6
Rutgers ‡	98	69,319	71,747	70,062	73,488	36,469	44,523	19.0
Saskatchewan †	38	55,404	58,792	53,606	56,183	31,123	33,453	16.8
South Carolina ‡	54	50,613	50,948	46,079	46,427	34,000	34,000	17.1
Southern California ‡	101	65,332	73,042	59,625	63,100	45,000	45,000	18.5
Southern Illinois	39	54,850	54,339	47,968	46,735	38,200	39,000	14.9
SUNY Albany ‡	57	55,143	56,556	53,758	55,285	37,500	37,500	18.3
SUNY Buffalo ‡	102	54,022	56,563	50,336	52,913	38,000	38,753	13.5
SUNY Stony Brook ‡	28	67,421	64,731	63,135	62,387	41,000	41,000	20.3
Syracuse ‡	46	57,948	59,142	52,063	53,675	35,000	36,000	19.2
Temple	40	53,081	58,513	48,194	52,688	34,000	36,500	18.1
Tennessee ‡	48	59,006	60,843	55,466	56,564	36,500	40,000	15.5
Texas ‡	128	58,726	59,768	53,729	54,736	38,000	40,000	16.5
Texas A&M ‡	86	54,218	55,163	48,543	49,950	40,000	40,000	14.6
Texas Tech ‡	57	51,482	51,426	46,139	46,973	38,000	38,000	11.5
Toronto †‡	144	58,020	63,296	61,362	65,454	33,500	36,649	16.8
Tulane ‡	37	53,398	55,000	51,572	53,120	34,000	34,000	16.9
Utah	50	51,561	53,434	48,000	49,117	37,000	38,000	18.0
Vanderbilt ‡	57	49,818	54,619	46,534	50,131	34,000	36,000	17.8
Virginia ‡	67	58,239	61,920	55,600	60,050	39,000	40,000	16.7
Virginia Tech	32	55,211	57,304	52,828	55,968	35,000	38,000	18.0
Washington ‡	97	58,113	59,273	53,724	54,798	38,000	38,800	19.9
Washington State	45	52,412	59,010	50,917	57,647	33,000	37,000	19.7
Washington U.-St.Louis ‡	49	57,064	58,839	49,259	50,863	37,000	37,000	18.7
Waterloo †‡	33	52,229	58,147	53,013	59,827	30,163	33,491	20.0
Wayne State ‡	93	59,880	50,166	52,481	44,598	39,000	36,000	10.2
Western Ontario †‡	64	44,131	48,647	42,281	46,456	33,753	37,185	14.2
Wisconsin ‡	144	56,918	57,610	54,544	55,391	36,968	37,719	17.5
Yale	207	69,748	68,596	63,532	61,096	44,400	40,400	17.7
York †‡	55	62,777	69,150	61,594	64,312	31,435	33,788	16.4

*Directors are included in figures for average years of experience and filled positions, but not in either the average or median salary statistics. Excludes medical and law libraries. See Tables 35 and 42 for statistics related to medical and law library salaries.

† Canadian salaries expressed in U.S. dollars.

‡ See Footnotes.

TABLE 8: BEGINNING PROFESSIONAL SALARIES IN ARL UNIVERSITY LIBRARIES
RANK ORDER TABLE, FY 2004-05*

Rank	Institution	Salary	Rank	Institution	Salary
1	Johns Hopkins	$47,680	58	Duke	$36,850
2	Columbia	45,700	59	Hawaii	36,727
3	Connecticut	45,000	60	Purdue	36,500
3	New York	45,000	60	Tennessee	36,500
3	Southern California	45,000	62	Rutgers	36,469
6	Yale	44,400	63	Florida State	36,000
7	MIT	43,800	63	Houston	36,000
8	Arizona	43,118	63	Illinois, Chicago	36,000
9	Kent State	42,778	63	Kentucky	36,000
10	Chicago	42,650	63	Miami	36,000
11	Brigham Young	42,300	63	Minnesota	36,000
12	Harvard	42,100	63	Notre Dame	36,000
13	Illinois, Urbana	42,000	63	Rochester	36,000
14	Michigan State	41,000	71	Indiana	35,869
14	SUNY Stony Brook	41,000	72	Howard	35,049
16	Auburn	40,930	73	Alabama	35,000
17	Cornell	40,000	73	Case Western Reserve	35,000
17	Florida	40,000	73	Emory	35,000
17	Georgetown	40,000	73	Iowa	35,000
17	Georgia Tech	40,000	73	Kansas	35,000
17	Maryland	40,000	73	Louisiana State	35,000
17	Nebraska	40,000	73	Louisville	35,000
17	North Carolina State	40,000	73	Michigan	35,000
17	Pennsylvania	40,000	73	Syracuse	35,000
17	Princeton	40,000	73	Virginia Tech	35,000
17	Texas A&M	40,000	83	Brown	34,650
27	New Mexico	39,900	84	Rice	34,527
28	Ohio State	39,500	85	Northwestern	34,000
29	Colorado State	39,000	85	Oklahoma State	34,000
29	Delaware	39,000	85	Oregon	34,000
29	Oklahoma	39,000	85	South Carolina	34,000
29	Virginia	39,000	85	Temple	34,000
29	Wayne State	39,000	85	Tulane	34,000
34	Pennsylvania State	38,500	85	Vanderbilt	34,000
35	Southern Illinois	38,200	92	Western Ontario	33,753
36	Arizona State	38,000	93	Toronto	33,500
36	Colorado	38,000	94	British Columbia	33,277
36	George Washington	38,000	95	Cincinnati	33,000
36	Iowa State	38,000	95	Ohio	33,000
36	SUNY Buffalo	38,000	95	Washington State	33,000
36	Texas	38,000	98	Alberta	32,689
36	Texas Tech	38,000	99	Boston University	32,000
36	Washington	38,000	99	Georgia	32,000
44	Calif. Berkeley	37,920	99	Missouri	32,000
44	Calif. Davis	37,920	102	Laval	31,775
44	Calif. Irvine	37,920	103	Manitoba	31,688
44	Calif. Los Angeles	37,920	104	York	31,435
44	Calif. Riverside	37,920	105	Queen's	31,378
44	Calif. San Diego	37,920	106	Saskatchewan	31,123
44	Calif. Santa Barbara	37,920	107	Guelph	30,662
51	Boston College	37,550	108	McGill	30,522
52	North Carolina	37,500	109	Waterloo	30,163
52	SUNY Albany	37,500	110	Pittsburgh	30,000
54	Massachusetts	37,274	111	Montreal	29,971
55	Utah	37,000	112	McMaster	29,488
55	Washington-St. Louis	37,000	113	Dartmouth	28,119
57	Wisconsin	36,968			

* Reprinted from *ARL Annual Salary Survey 2004-05*. Beginning salary figures represent officially designated base, not necessarily salaries of actual incumbents. Excludes medical and law libraries. See Tables 36 and 43 for statistics related to medical and law library salaries.

‡ Canadian salaries expressed in U.S. dollars.

TABLE 9: BEGINNING PROFESSIONAL SALARIES IN ARL UNIVERSITY LIBRARIES
RANK ORDER TABLE, FY 2005-06*

Rank	Institution	Salary	Rank	Institution	Salary
1	Kent State	$48,889	57	Calif. Davis	$37,920
2	Connecticut	48,000	57	Calif. Irvine	37,920
3	Columbia	47,500	57	Calif. Los Angeles	37,920
4	New York	47,000	57	Calif. San Diego	37,920
5	North Carolina State	45,000	57	Calif. Santa Barbara	37,920
5	Southern California	45,000	63	Wisconsin	37,719
7	Rutgers	44,523	64	Kentucky	37,500
8	Georgia Tech	44,000	64	SUNY Albany	37,500
8	MIT	44,000	66	Massachusetts	37,274
10	Chicago	43,930	67	Western Ontario	37,185
11	Harvard	43,600	68	Dartmouth	37,000
12	Johns Hopkins	43,113	68	Emory	37,000
13	Brigham Young	43,100	68	Houston	37,000
14	Michigan State	43,000	68	Washington State	37,000
15	Auburn	42,570	68	Washington-St. Louis	37,000
16	Florida	42,000	73	Duke	36,850
16	George Washington	42,000	74	Hawaii	36,720
16	Georgetown	42,000	75	Toronto	36,649
16	Illinois, Chicago	42,000	76	Temple	36,500
16	Illinois, Urbana	42,000	77	Alberta	36,366
16	Purdue	42,000	78	Indiana	36,227
22	Arizona	41,688	79	Louisville	36,000
23	Cornell	41,600	79	Minnesota	36,000
24	SUNY Stony Brook	41,000	79	Northwestern	36,000
25	Calif. Riverside	40,560	79	Notre Dame	36,000
26	Nebraska	40,500	79	Rochester	36,000
27	Yale	40,400	79	Syracuse	36,000
28	Colorado	40,000	79	Vanderbilt	36,000
28	Iowa	40,000	79	Wayne State	36,000
28	Iowa State	40,000	87	Louisiana State	35,800
28	Kansas	40,000	88	British Columbia	35,768
28	Maryland	40,000	89	Brown	35,500
28	Michigan	40,000	90	Manitoba	35,083
28	New Mexico	40,000	91	Howard	35,049
28	North Carolina	40,000	92	Alabama	35,000
28	Ohio State	40,000	92	Case Western Reserve	35,000
28	Oklahoma	40,000	92	Cincinnati	35,000
28	Pennsylvania	40,000	92	Oregon	35,000
28	Princeton	40,000	96	Queen's	34,738
28	Tennessee	40,000	97	Rice	34,527
28	Texas	40,000	98	Laval	34,154
28	Texas A&M	40,000	99	Oklahoma State	34,000
28	Virginia	40,000	99	South Carolina	34,000
44	Colorado State	39,000	99	Tulane	34,000
44	Delaware	39,000	102	York	33,788
44	Pennsylvania State	39,000	103	Guelph	33,781
44	Southern Illinois	39,000	104	Waterloo	33,491
48	Washington	38,800	105	Saskatchewan	33,453
49	SUNY Buffalo	38,753	106	Montreal	33,241
50	Boston College	38,700	107	Boston University	33,000
51	Arizona State	38,000	107	Ohio	33,000
51	Florida State	38,000	109	McGill	32,808
51	Miami	38,000	110	McMaster	32,646
51	Texas Tech	38,000	111	Missouri	32,500
51	Utah	38,000	112	Georgia	32,000
51	Virginia Tech	38,000	113	Pittsburgh	30,000
57	Calif. Berkeley	37,920			

* Beginning salary figures represent officially designated base, not necessarily salaries of actual incumbents. Excludes medical and law libraries. See Tables 36 and 43 for statistics related to medical and law library salaries.

† See Footnotes.

‡ Canadian salaries expressed in U.S. dollars.

TABLE 10: MEDIAN PROFESSIONAL SALARIES IN ARL UNIVERSITY LIBRARIES
RANK ORDER TABLE, FY 2004-05*

Rank	Institution	Salary	Rank	Institution	Salary
1	California, Los Angeles	$71,592	58	Saskatchewan	$53,606
2	California, Berkeley	70,500	59	Minnesota	53,603
2	California, Davis	70,500	60	Michigan	53,349
4	Rutgers	70,062	61	Miami	53,233
5	California, Irvine	69,365	62	Iowa State	53,114
6	California, Santa Barbara	67,592	63	Waterloo	53,013
7	Massachusetts	66,437	64	North Carolina State	52,852
8	New Mexico	66,226	65	Virginia Tech	52,828
9	California, San Diego	65,000	66	North Carolina	52,750
10	California, Riverside	64,164	67	Wayne State	52,481
11	Yale	63,532	68	Ohio State	52,277
12	Dartmouth	63,521	69	Illinois, Urbana	52,265
13	SUNY Stony Brook	63,135	70	Arizona	52,181
14	Connecticut	62,981	71	Kansas	52,135
15	Princeton	62,700	72	Syracuse	52,063
16	York	61,594	73	Laval	51,828
17	Toronto	61,362	74	Kent State	51,758
18	Alberta	61,316	75	Illinois, Chicago	51,693
19	Chicago	61,082	76	Arizona State	51,628
20	Delaware	61,007	77	Tulane	51,572
21	Harvard	59,845	78	Iowa	50,939
22	Manitoba	59,837	79	Washington State	50,917
23	New York University	59,782	80	Auburn	50,865
24	Southern California	59,625	81	McMaster	50,764
25	Notre Dame	59,281	82	Purdue	50,600
26	George Washington	58,650	83	Nebraska	50,402
27	Columbia	58,500	84	SUNY Buffalo	50,336
28	MIT	58,200	85	Pittsburgh	50,324
29	Brown	58,069	86	Case Western Reserve	50,293
30	Pennsylvania State	57,912	87	Oregon	49,607
31	Colorado State	57,650	88	Washington U.-St. Louis	49,259
32	Northwestern	57,493	89	Rice	49,113
33	Indiana	57,281	90	Guelph	48,596
34	Georgetown	57,214	91	Texas A&M	48,543
35	Boston College	56,750	92	Temple	48,194
35	Michigan State	56,750	93	Utah	48,000
37	Emory	56,100	94	Southern Illinois	47,968
38	Louisville	55,908	95	Kentucky	47,864
39	Hawaii	55,872	96	Georgia	47,278
40	Virginia	55,600	97	Montreal	47,060
41	Pennsylvania	55,575	98	Boston University	46,800
42	Tennessee	55,466	99	Vanderbilt	46,534
43	Brigham Young	55,390	100	Missouri	46,431
44	Colorado	55,362	101	Texas Tech	46,139
45	Cincinnati	55,128	102	South Carolina	46,079
46	Maryland	55,083	103	Florida	45,971
47	Georgia Tech	55,080	104	Howard	45,828
48	Cornell	55,000	105	Rochester	45,557
48	Johns Hopkins	55,000	106	Houston	43,490
50	McGill	54,653	107	Ohio University	43,113
51	Queen's	54,609	108	Western Ontario	42,281
52	Wisconsin	54,544	109	Alabama	42,145
53	Duke	54,050	110	Oklahoma	41,644
54	SUNY Albany	53,758	111	Louisiana State	41,444
55	Texas	53,729	112	Florida State	41,128
56	Washington	53,724	113	Oklahoma State	40,236
57	British Columbia	53,663			

* Reprinted from *ARL Annual Salary Survey 2004-05*. Salaries of directors are not included in the calculation of medians.
    Excludes medical and law libraries. See Tables 37 and 44 for statistics related to medical and law library salaries.
† See Footnotes.
‡ Canadian salaries expressed in U.S. dollars.

TABLE 11: MEDIAN PROFESSIONAL SALARIES IN ARL UNIVERSITY LIBRARIES
RANK ORDER TABLE, FY 2005-06*

Rank	Institution	Salary	Rank	Institution	Salary
1	California, Berkeley	$75,480	58	Guelph	$55,570
2	Rutgers	73,488	59	Purdue	55,535
3	California, Davis	70,500	60	McMaster	55,520
3	California, Irvine	70,500	61	Pittsburgh	55,414
3	California, Los Angeles	70,500	62	Wisconsin	55,391
6	Alberta	67,656	63	Miami	55,349
7	Princeton	67,300	64	SUNY Albany	55,285
8	Connecticut	66,666	65	Kansas	55,244
9	New Mexico	66,598	66	Auburn	55,175
10	Manitoba	66,036	67	British Columbia	55,141
11	Massachusetts	65,640	68	Ohio State	54,911
12	Toronto	65,454	69	Arizona State	54,866
13	California, San Diego	65,000	70	Washington	54,798
14	York	64,312	71	Iowa State	54,751
15	California, Santa Barbara	64,164	72	Texas	54,736
16	Dartmouth	63,704	73	Laval	54,639
17	Chicago	63,318	74	Duke	54,400
18	Delaware	63,314	75	Illinois, Urbana	54,213
19	Southern California	63,100	76	North Carolina State	54,174
20	SUNY Stony Brook	62,387	77	Arizona	54,053
21	MIT	62,100	78	Syracuse	53,675
22	Harvard	61,987	79	Case Western Reserve	53,500
23	New York University	61,765	80	Tulane	53,120
24	California, Riverside	61,724	81	Iowa	53,001
25	Queen`s	61,342	82	SUNY Buffalo	52,913
26	Louisville	61,114	83	Kentucky	52,785
27	Yale	61,096	84	Temple	52,688
28	Virginia	60,050	85	Illinois, Chicago	51,764
29	Waterloo	59,827	86	Georgia Tech	51,497
30	Minnesota	59,776	87	Rice	51,100
31	Columbia	59,530	88	Oregon	50,980
32	Pennsylvania State	59,436	89	Washington U.-St. Louis	50,863
33	Notre Dame	59,380	90	Montreal	50,583
34	George Washington	58,650	91	Florida	50,282
35	Boston College	58,625	92	Vanderbilt	50,131
36	McGill	58,588	93	Texas A&M	49,950
37	Brown	58,573	94	Kent State	49,470
38	Northwestern	58,397	95	Nebraska	49,357
39	Hawaii	58,068	96	Utah	49,117
40	Georgetown	58,017	97	Howard	48,956
41	Cincinnati	57,929	98	Boston University	48,900
42	Michigan State	57,800	99	Rochester	48,339
43	Cornell	57,768	100	Alabama	48,114
44	Washington State	57,647	101	Georgia	48,023
45	Michigan	57,527	102	Missouri	47,559
46	Emory	57,525	103	Oklahoma State	47,376
47	Brigham Young	57,500	104	Oklahoma	47,210
48	Johns Hopkins	57,355	105	Texas Tech	46,973
49	Pennsylvania	57,233	106	Southern Illinois	46,735
50	Colorado	56,837	107	Western Ontario	46,456
51	Tennessee	56,564	108	South Carolina	46,427
52	Saskatchewan	56,183	109	Florida State	44,853
53	Colorado State	56,150	110	Wayne State	44,598
54	Indiana	56,000	111	Ohio University	43,864
55	Virginia Tech	55,968	112	Houston	42,363
56	Maryland	55,848	113	Louisiana State	40,188
57	North Carolina	55,650			

* Salaries of directors are not included in the calculation of medians. Excludes medical and law libraries. See Tables 37 and 44 for statistics related to medical and law library salaries.
† Canadian salaries expressed in U.S. dollars.

TABLE 12: AVERAGE PROFESSIONAL SALARIES IN ARL UNIVERSITY LIBRARIES
RANK ORDER TABLE, FY 2004-05*

Rank	Institution	Salary	Rank	Institution	Salary
1	California, Berkeley	$72,651	58	Manitoba	$57,169
2	California, Los Angeles	72,036	59	Washington U.-St. Louis	57,064
3	Yale	69,748	60	Purdue	57,050
4	Rutgers	69,319	61	Wisconsin	56,918
5	Princeton	68,399	62	Kansas	56,913
6	California, Davis	68,339	63	North Carolina	56,872
7	Connecticut	68,254	64	Ohio State	56,375
8	California, Irvine	68,236	65	Minnesota	56,176
9	California, Santa Barbara	67,563	66	Pittsburgh	55,963
10	California, San Diego	67,498	67	Miami	55,431
11	SUNY Stony Brook	67,421	68	Saskatchewan	55,404
12	Chicago	66,642	69	Georgia Tech	55,274
13	New York University	66,510	70	Virginia Tech	55,211
14	Columbia	65,991	71	Rice	55,150
15	Massachusetts	65,949	72	SUNY Albany	55,143
16	New Mexico	65,770	73	British Columbia	55,038
17	Southern California	65,332	74	Queen`s	54,936
18	Harvard	64,912	75	Nebraska	54,905
19	Dartmouth	64,221	76	Southern Illinois	54,850
20	California, Riverside	64,091	77	Iowa	54,776
21	MIT	63,513	78	Iowa State	54,419
22	Delaware	62,936	79	Texas A&M	54,218
23	York	62,777	80	Kent State	54,216
24	George Washington	61,687	81	SUNY Buffalo	54,022
25	Cornell	61,673	82	Auburn	53,850
26	Georgetown	61,195	83	Tulane	53,398
27	Pennsylvania State	61,145	84	Case Western Reserve	53,387
28	Notre Dame	61,008	85	Arizona State	53,217
29	Boston College	60,321	86	Temple	53,081
30	Brown	60,107	87	Oregon	52,516
31	Indiana	60,025	88	Washington State	52,412
32	Wayne State	59,880	89	Waterloo	52,229
33	Michigan State	59,803	90	McGill	52,073
34	Johns Hopkins	59,759	91	Missouri	52,059
35	Northwestern	59,657	92	McMaster	51,882
36	Tennessee	59,006	93	Utah	51,561
37	Colorado State	59,003	94	Texas Tech	51,482
38	Emory	58,976	95	Georgia	50,847
39	Michigan	58,856	96	Kentucky	50,800
40	Arizona	58,848	97	Guelph	50,616
41	Texas	58,726	98	South Carolina	50,613
42	Pennsylvania	58,659	99	Boston University	50,242
43	Cincinnati	58,623	100	Vanderbilt	49,818
44	Alberta	58,593	101	Florida	49,742
45	Illinois, Urbana	58,423	102	Houston	49,319
46	Duke	58,328	103	Howard	48,931
47	Virginia	58,239	104	Ohio University	48,881
48	Washington	58,113	105	Laval	48,698
49	Toronto	58,020	106	Rochester	47,775
50	Syracuse	57,948	107	Montreal	47,396
51	Maryland	57,943	108	Alabama	45,900
52	North Carolina State	57,932	109	Oklahoma	45,724
53	Illinois, Chicago	57,712	110	Florida State	45,588
54	Brigham Young	57,637	111	Louisiana State	44,141
55	Louisville	57,383	112	Western Ontario	44,131
56	Hawaii	57,357	113	Oklahoma State	43,972
57	Colorado	57,212			

* Reprinted from *ARL Annual Salary Survey 2004-05*. Salaries of directors are not included in the calculation of averages.
Excludes medical and law libraries. See Tables 38 and 45 for statistics related to medical and law library salaries.
† See Footnotes.
‡ Canadian salaries expressed in U.S. dollars.

TABLE 13: AVERAGE PROFESSIONAL SALARIES IN ARL UNIVERSITY LIBRARIES
RANK ORDER TABLE, FY 2005-06*

Rank	Institution	Salary	Rank	Institution	Salary
1	California, Berkeley	$74,847	58	Kansas	$59,314
2	Southern California	73,042	59	Washington	59,273
3	California, Los Angeles	72,477	60	Maryland	59,218
4	Princeton	71,845	61	Syracuse	59,142
5	Rutgers	71,747	62	Washington State	59,010
6	Connecticut	71,115	63	Colorado	59,006
7	California, Davis	69,263	64	Washington U.-St. Louis	58,839
8	New York University	69,214	65	Saskatchewan	58,792
9	York	69,150	66	Iowa	58,742
10	Yale	68,596	67	Temple	58,513
11	California, San Diego	68,199	68	Duke	58,326
12	New Mexico	68,175	69	Waterloo	58,147
13	California, Irvine	67,817	70	Ohio State	57,760
14	California, Santa Barbara	67,798	71	Wisconsin	57,610
15	Chicago	67,795	72	Rice	57,524
16	Harvard	67,247	73	Illinois, Chicago	57,470
17	Columbia	66,788	74	British Columbia	57,426
18	Dartmouth	66,275	75	Virginia Tech	57,304
19	Delaware	65,175	76	Guelph	57,165
20	Massachusetts	65,120	77	Georgia Tech	57,097
21	MIT	65,006	78	Auburn	56,868
22	SUNY Stony Brook	64,731	79	McGill	56,669
23	Cornell	64,443	80	SUNY Buffalo	56,563
24	Manitoba	63,923	81	SUNY Albany	56,556
25	California, Riverside	63,730	82	Nebraska	56,297
26	Michigan	63,448	83	Iowa State	56,262
27	Toronto	63,296	84	Arizona State	56,240
28	Alberta	63,237	85	McMaster	55,735
29	Minnesota	62,872	86	Florida	55,378
30	Pennsylvania State	62,619	87	Case Western Reserve	55,194
31	Boston College	62,260	88	Texas A&M	55,163
32	Georgetown	62,118	89	Tulane	55,000
33	Virginia	61,920	90	Oregon	54,627
34	Notre Dame	61,908	91	Vanderbilt	54,619
35	George Washington	61,800	92	Southern Illinois	54,339
36	Brown	61,624	93	Kentucky	54,086
37	Northwestern	61,459	94	Utah	53,434
38	Queen`s	61,355	95	Boston University	52,555
39	Johns Hopkins	61,259	96	Georgia	52,547
40	Arizona	61,122	97	Alabama	52,161
41	Cincinnati	61,054	98	Missouri	51,922
42	Illinois, Urbana	60,878	99	Texas Tech	51,426
43	Tennessee	60,843	100	Oklahoma State	51,414
44	Purdue	60,839	101	Rochester	51,184
45	Louisville	60,837	102	Howard	51,033
46	Emory	60,657	103	Montreal	50,998
47	Pennsylvania	60,456	104	South Carolina	50,948
48	North Carolina State	60,293	105	Kent State	50,491
49	Michigan State	60,069	106	Oklahoma	50,372
50	North Carolina	59,769	107	Wayne State	50,166
51	Texas	59,768	108	Laval	50,058
52	Hawaii	59,748	109	Florida State	48,890
53	Colorado State	59,725	110	Ohio University	48,769
54	Brigham Young	59,699	111	Western Ontario	48,647
55	Indiana	59,557	112	Houston	47,115
56	Miami	59,425	113	Louisiana State	43,882
57	Pittsburgh	59,357			

* Salaries of directors are not included in the calculation of averages.

    Excludes medical and law libraries. See Tables 38 and 45 for statistics related to medical and law library salaries.

    † Canadian salaries expressed in U.S. dollars.

TABLE 14: AVERAGE, MEDIAN, AND BEGINNING PROFESSIONAL SALARIES
IN ARL UNIVERSITY LIBRARIES
SUMMARY OF RANKINGS, FYs 2002-03 TO 2005-06*

Institution	Average Salaries				Median Salaries				Beginning Salaries			
FY	2003	2004	2005	2006	2003	2004	2005	2006	2003	2004	2005	2006
Alabama	106	112	108	97	113	113	109	100	93	97	73	92
Alberta	103	89	44	28	82	56	18	6	104	104	98	77
Arizona	66	37	40	40	65	64	70	77	4	7	8	22
Arizona State	64	75	85	84	43	57	76	69	38	30	36	51
Auburn	75	62	82	78	67	63	80	66	16	11	16	15
Boston University	88	90	99	95	96	99	98	98	86	96	99	107
Boston College	26	27	29	31	28	33	35	35	49	52	51	50
Brigham Young	27	23	54	54	23	18	43	47	15	14	11	13
British Columbia	107	105	73	74	103	97	57	67	111	112	94	88
Brown	24	26	30	36	27	25	29	37	62	75	83	89
California, Berkeley	1	1	1	1	2	2	2	1	25	38	44	57
Californis, Davis	4	5	6	7	2	2	2	3	25	38	44	57
California, Irvine	7	8	8	13	4	5	5	3	25	38	44	57
California, Los Angeles	2	2	2	3	1	1	1	3	25	38	44	57
California, Riverside	14	19	20	25	10	8	10	24	25	38	44	25
California, San Diego	6	6	10	11	6	6	9	13	25	38	44	57
California, Santa Barbara	9	9	9	14	8	8	6	15	25	38	44	57
Case Western Reserve	74	76	84	87	55	81	86	79	78	15	73	92
Chicago	17	10	12	15	16	13	19	17	10	10	10	10
Cincinnati	54	43	43	41	52	26	45	41	86	84	95	92
Colorado	31	49	57	63	31	36	44	50	60	74	36	28
Colorado State	25	53	37	53	20	39	31	53	18	29	29	44
Columbia	11	11	14	17	17	23	27	31	3	4	2	3
Connecticut	8	12	7	6	9	10	14	8	5	2	3	2
Cornell	23	25	25	23	38	40	48	43	33	25	17	23
Dartmouth	18	20	19	18	14	21	12	16	62	75	113	68
Delaware	29	21	22	19	26	14	20	18	33	25	29	44
Duke	43	40	46	68	48	44	53	74	44	53	58	73
Emory	30	29	38	46	24	22	37	46	79	62	73	68
Florida	93	95	101	86	94	96	103	91	53	16	17	16
Florida State	98	102	110	109	99	107	112	109	86	92	63	51
George Washington	35	33	24	35	32	38	26	34	20	30	36	16
Georgetown	48	28	26	32	40	35	34	40	19	16	17	16
Georgia	72	80	95	96	73	80	96	101	94	99	99	112
Georgia Tech	68	66	69	77	50	46	47	86	20	25	17	8
Guelph	112	109	97	76	112	106	90	58	106	106	107	103
Harvard	15	15	18	16	13	17	21	22	48	13	12	11
Hawaii	56	54	56	52	41	37	39	39	50	59	59	74
Houston	96	98	102	112	108	108	106	112	62	62	63	68
Howard	90	94	103	102	88	94	104	97	52	61	72	91
Illinois, Chicago	83	51	53	73	81	68	75	85	62	62	63	16
Illinois, Urbana	50	39	45	42	68	61	69	75	17	16	13	16

* Excludes medical and law libraries.
† Not a member during this year.

TABLE 14: AVERAGE, MEDIAN, AND BEGINNING PROFESSIONAL SALARIES
IN ARL UNIVERSITY LIBRARIES
SUMMARY OF RANKINGS, FYs 2002-03 TO 2005-06*

Institution	Average Salaries				Median Salaries				Beginning Salaries			
FY	2003	2004	2005	2006	2003	2004	2005	2006	2003	2004	2005	2006
Indiana	21	32	31	55	29	29	33	54	59	60	71	78
Iowa	34	41	77	66	39	53	78	81	86	62	73	28
Iowa State	76	82	78	83	56	55	62	71	62	30	36	28
Johns Hopkins	28	22	34	39	36	30	48	48	7	9	1	12
Kansas	82	68	62	58	85	84	71	65	62	62	73	28
Kent State	39	48	80	105	37	47	74	94	8	6	9	1
Kentucky	91	84	96	93	92	85	95	83	62	54	63	64
Laval	111	111	105	108	98	95	73	73	103	102	102	98
Louisiana State	108	107	111	113	110	110	111	113	62	75	73	87
Louisville	47	38	55	45	34	24	38	26	53	75	73	79
McGill	110	110	90	79	97	93	50	36	114	111	108	109
McMaster	109	106	92	85	109	103	81	60	110	109	112	110
Manitoba	102	97	58	24	89	70	22	10	113	114	103	90
Maryland	40	47	51	60	46	42	46	56	14	16	17	28
Massachusetts	22	35	15	20	21	28	7	11	51	98	54	66
MIT	16	13	21	21	17	19	28	21	9	5	7	8
Miami	69	96	67	56	42	78	61	63	86	92	63	51
Michigan	36	44	39	26	51	58	60	45	53	62	73	28
Michigan State	45	34	33	49	47	33	35	42	33	16	14	14
Minnesota	53	56	65	29	44	51	59	30	53	62	63	79
Missouri	92	92	91	98	106	102	100	102	97	92	99	111
Montreal	113	113	107	103	111	112	97	90	109	107	111	106
Nebraska	44	74	75	82	60	75	83	95	60	49	17	26
New Mexico	12	17	16	12	11	12	8	9	79	30	27	28
New York	58	42	13	8	59	49	23	23	5	8	3	4
North Carolina	67	78	63	50	62	82	66	57	62	75	52	28
North Carolina State	57	52	52	48	70	69	64	76	38	25	17	5
Northwestern	37	31	35	37	35	32	32	38	86	91	85	79
Notre Dame	32	24	28	34	25	15	25	33	62	62	63	79
Ohio University	85	86	104	110	84	90	107	111	79	84	95	107
Ohio State	71	71	64	70	71	66	68	68	46	23	28	28
Oklahoma	94	103	109	106	100	111	110	104	33	46	29	28
Oklahoma State	100	104	113	100	102	105	113	103	79	84	85	99
Oregon	87	85	87	90	90	91	87	88	79	84	85	92
Pennsylvania	52	46	42	47	53	48	41	49	12	16	17	28
Pennsylvania State	33	30	27	30	33	31	30	32	20	30	34	44
Pittsburgh	63	60	66	57	77	76	85	61	97	84	110	113
Princeton	10	7	5	4	12	11	15	7	38	23	17	28
Purdue	70	67	60	44	80	77	82	59	94	92	60	16
Queen's	104	100	74	38	105	98	51	25	105	105	105	96
Rice	60	65	71	72	74	71	89	87	77	83	84	97
Rochester	97	99	106	101	104	104	105	99	53	54	63	79

* Excludes medical and law libraries.
† Not a member during this year.

37

TABLE 14: AVERAGE, MEDIAN, AND BEGINNING PROFESSIONAL SALARIES
IN ARL UNIVERSITY LIBRARIES
SUMMARY OF RANKINGS, FYs 2002-03 TO 2005-06*

Institution	Average Salaries				Median Salaries				Beginning Salaries			
FY	2003	2004	2005	2006	2003	2004	2005	2006	2003	2004	2005	2006
Rutgers	5	4	4	5	5	4	4	2	37	51	62	7
Saskatchewan	95	93	68	65	86	79	58	52	108	110	106	105
South Carolina	89	91	98	104	93	100	102	108	97	99	85	99
Southern California	13	14	17	2	19	27	24	19	2	2	3	5
Southern Illinois	59	63	76	92	83	83	94	106	20	30	35	44
SUNY Albany	73	73	72	81	76	62	54	64	32	45	52	64
SUNY Buffalo	55	69	81	80	61	74	84	82	20	30	36	49
SUNY Stony Brook	19	18	11	22	15	16	13	20	12	16	14	24
Syracuse	61	55	50	61	72	65	72	78	62	62	73	79
Temple	77	77	86	67	91	86	92	84	62	75	85	76
Tennessee	49	36	36	43	57	41	42	51	79	62	60	28
Texas	42	61	41	51	54	72	55	72	38	54	36	28
Texas A&M	78	79	79	88	95	92	91	93	46	30	17	28
Texas Tech	101	101	94	99	107	109	101	105	38	54	36	51
Toronto	99	88	49	27	66	45	17	12	112	113	93	75
Tulane	80	72	83	89	75	60	77	80	62	75	85	99
Utah	79	83	93	94	79	87	93	96	62	54	55	51
Vanderbilt	81	87	100	91	87	88	99	92	86	84	85	79
Virginia	38	58	47	33	30	50	40	28	62	62	29	28
Virginia Tech	65	64	70	75	58	59	65	55	85	75	73	51
Washington	46	50	48	59	49	52	56	70	53	46	36	48
Washington State	84	81	88	62	64	67	79	44	97	84	95	68
Washington U.-St. Louis	62	59	59	64	78	89	88	89	94	62	55	68
Waterloo	105	108	89	69	101	101	63	29	107	108	109	104
Wayne State	41	45	32	107	69	73	67	110	38	46	29	79
Western Ontario	114	114	112	111	114	114	108	107	101	101	92	67
Wisconsin	51	57	61	71	45	43	52	62	45	50	57	63
Yale	20	16	3	10	22	20	11	27	11	12	6	27
York	86	70	23	9	63	54	16	14	102	103	104	102

* Excludes medical and law libraries.
† Not a member during this year.

TABLE 15: DISTRIBUTION OF PROFESSIONAL STAFF IN ARL UNIVERSITY LIBRARIES BY SALARY AND POSITION, FY 2005-06*

SALARY INTERVALS	NUMBER OF STAFF								PERCENTAGE AT EACH LEVEL †							
	Dir.	Assoc. Dir.	Asst. Dir.	Branch Head	Subj. Spec.	Func. Spec.	Dept. Head	Other Prof.	Dir.	Assoc. Dir.	Asst. Dir.	Branch Head	Subj. Spec.	Func. Spec.	Dept. Head	Other Prof.
$250,000 and above	8		1						7		1					
200,000-249,999	14			1					13			0				
175,000-199,999	16	3	1					1	14	1	1					0
150,000-174,999	32	8		1			1		29	3		0			0	
140,000-149,999	18	4	2				1		16	2	1				0	
130,000-139,999	9	8	5	2	1		2		8	3	3	0	0		0	
120,000-129,999	3	12	6	3	4		1	2	3	5	3	1	0		1	0
110,000-119,999	6	40	10	6	6	1	13		5	16	5	1	0	0	1	
100,000-109,999	4	49	32	15	15	4	24	7	4	20	17	3	1	0	2	0
95,000-99,999		26	23	9	11	7	22	8		10	12	2	1	1	2	0
90,000-94,999	2	35	20	22	18	5	41	7	2	14	10	4	1	1	3	0
85,000-89,999		22	24	31	30	20	62	20		9	13	6	2	2	4	1
80,000-84,999		16	22	45	42	49	99	48		6	12	8	2	5	7	2
76,000-79,999		13	10	32	53	29	104	47		5	5	6	3	3	7	2
74,000-75,999		3	3	29	35	24	65	24		1	2	5	2	2	4	1
72,000-73,999		1	4	22	43	19	70	33		0	2	4	3	2	5	1
70,000-71,999		1	1	22	46	40	89	56		0	1	4	3	4	6	2
68,000-69,999		1	7	29	42	20	64	46		0	4	5	2	2	4	2
66,000-67,999		2	2	31	48	23	81	60		1	1	6	3	2	6	2
64,000-65,999		2	5	27	55	42	87	84		1	3	5	3	4	6	3
62,000-63,999			1	27	67	41	61	78			1	5	4	4	4	3
60,000-61,999			2	30	75	55	84	106			1	6	4	6	6	4
58,000-59,999			1	18	72	61	57	128			1	3	4	6	4	5
56,000-57,999			1	17	84	79	77	143			1	3	5	8	5	5
54,000-55,999		1	1	24	93	61	66	153		0	1	5	6	6	5	5
52,000-53,999		2	2	17	94	77	51	183		1	1	3	6	8	4	7
50,000-51,999		1		20	94	61	41	225		0		4	6	6	3	8
48,000-49,999			1	12	107	44	40	212			1	2	6	5	3	8
46,000-47,999			2	9	82	63	37	220			1	2	5	6	3	8
44,000-45,999				9	110	59	37	207				2	7	6	3	7
42,000-43,999			2	4	101	36	34	211			1	1	6	4	2	8
40,000-41,999				10	88	20	17	190				2	5	2	1	7
38,000-39,999				2	57	14	9	111				0	3	1	1	4
36,000-37,999				3	49	14	6	94				1	3	1	0	3
34,000-35,999				2	34	2	4	57				0	2	0	0	2
32,000-33,999					15	4	2	22					1	0	0	1
30,000-31,999					11	1	1	5					1	0	0	0
Less than 30,000					7		2	7					0		0	0
TOTAL	112	250	191	531	1,689	975	1,452	2,795	100%	100%	100%	100%	100%	100%	100%	100%

* Excludes medical and law libraries.
† A "0" percentage indicates less than one-half of one percent.

40

TABLE 16: DISTRIBUTION OF PROFESSIONAL STAFF IN ARL UNIVERSITY LIBRARIES BY SALARY, SEX, AND POSITION, FY 2005-06*

SALARY INTERVALS	Women								Men							
	Dir.	Assoc. Dir.	Asst. Dir.	Branch Head	Subj. Spec.	Func. Spec.	Dept. Head	Other Prof.	Dir.	Assoc. Dir.	Asst. Dir.	Branch Head	Subj. Spec.	Func. Spec.	Dept. Head	Other Prof.
$250,000 and above	3								5		1					
200,000-249,999	8								6			1				
175,000-199,999	10	2	1					1	6	1						
150,000-174,999	18	7							14	1		1				
140,000-149,999	14	3							4	1	2					
130,000-139,999	5	5	3				1		4	3	2	2	1			1
120,000-129,999	1	6	4	1				2	2	6	2	2	1		1	1
110,000-119,999	2	21	3	2	3		5		4	19	7	4	2	1	8	8
100,000-109,999	1	31	15	6	4	2	14	4	3	18	17	9	6	2	10	3
95,000-99,999		12	15	5	9	3	11	6		14	8	4	2	4	11	2
90,000-94,999	1	22	8	17	9	1	23	5	1	13	12	5	7	4	18	2
85,000-89,999		11	17	22	11	13	31	11		11	7	9	16	7	31	9
80,000-84,999		14	9	31	14	24	66	32		2	13	14	23	25	33	16
76,000-79,999		7	6	19	19	18	61	33		6	4	13	32	11	43	14
74,000-75,999		2	3	23	21	15	29	16		1		6	15	9	36	8
72,000-73,999		1	3	13	20	11	48	22			1	9	17	8	22	11
70,000-71,999				15	26	19	58	40		1	1	7	19	21	31	16
68,000-69,999		1	3	19	27	12	40	28			4	10	21	8	24	18
66,000-67,999		2		21	21	17	48	43			2	10	22	6	33	17
64,000-65,999		1	2	21	26	22	59	61		1	3	6	29	20	28	23
62,000-63,999			1	12	26	22	43	51				15	29	19	18	27
60,000-61,999			2	20	38	32	65	82				10	36	23	19	24
58,000-59,999				16	39	47	40	88			1	2	31	14	17	40
56,000-57,999		1		11	36	42	47	107			1	6	42	37	30	36
54,000-55,999			1	16	53	41	40	98				8	44	20	26	55
52,000-53,999			1	12	51	48	33	138		2	1	5	51	29	18	45
50,000-51,999				16	50	44	24	143				4	42	17	17	82
48,000-49,999		1	1	10	43	33	27	146				2	38	11	13	66
46,000-47,999			1	6	65	38	29	148		1	1	3	38	25	8	72
44,000-45,999				8	44	31	28	154				1	44	28	9	53
42,000-43,999			1	3	66	21	22	148			1	1	47	15	12	63
40,000-41,999				7	54	14	13	124				3	38	6	4	66
38,000-39,999				1	50	6	8	88		1		1	25	8	1	23
36,000-37,999				3	32	9	3	63					14	5	3	31
34,000-35,999				1	35	2	3	46				1	17		1	11
32,000-33,999					17	2	1	13					6	2	1	9
30,000-31,999					9		1	4					4	1		1
Less than 30,000					7		2	4					3			3
TOTAL	**63**	**150**	**100**	**357**	**929**	**589**	**923**	**1,949**	**49**	**100**	**91**	**174**	**760**	**386**	**529**	**846**

* Excludes medical and law libraries.

41

TABLE 17: NUMBER AND AVERAGE SALARIES OF ARL UNIVERSITY LIBRARIANS BY POSITION AND SEX, FY 2005-06*

Position		Women Salary	No.	Men Salary	No.	Total Salary	No.
Director		$168,146	63	$169,856	49	$168,894	112
Associate Director		102,989	150	101,725	100	102,484	250
Assistant Director		91,056	100	94,040	91	92,478	191
Head, Branch		68,289	357	74,057	174	70,179	531
Functional Specialist		56,140	929	56,921	760	56,491	1,689
Subject Specialist		58,227	589	59,854	386	58,871	975
Dept. Head:	Acquisitions	66,474	77	71,399	29	67,821	106
	Reference	70,076	87	68,569	38	69,618	125
	Cataloging	66,255	139	64,946	52	65,898	191
	Serials	61,434	30	65,551	8	62,301	38
	Documents/Maps	60,301	57	59,693	32	60,082	89
	Circulation	61,571	72	60,774	29	61,342	101
	Rare Books/Manuscripts	71,817	36	76,396	46	74,386	82
	Computer Systems	78,767	32	79,680	52	79,332	84
	Other	64,831	393	69,538	243	66,629	636
Reference:	Over 14 years experience	59,065	455	59,292	198	59,134	653
	10 to 14 years experience	51,980	152	50,027	68	51,377	220
	5 to 9 years experience	47,545	216	47,714	80	47,591	296
	Under 5 years experience	41,947	233	42,027	90	41,970	323
Cataloging:	Over 14 years experience	57,889	282	57,116	141	57,631	423
	10 to 14 years experience	48,175	64	51,850	35	49,474	99
	5 to 9 years experience	47,368	77	47,267	33	47,338	110
	Under 5 years experience	43,015	77	44,218	42	43,440	119
Other:	Over 14 years experience	62,978	172	63,271	66	63,060	238
	10 to 14 years experience	53,256	50	55,752	19	53,943	69
	5 to 9 years experience	47,664	83	46,530	37	47,314	120
	Under 5 years experience	42,616	88	46,015	37	43,622	125
All Positions		**$61,083**	**5,061**	**$63,984**	**2,935**	**$62,148**	**7,996**

* Canadian salaries expressed in U.S. dollars. See Table 32 for salaries of Canadian librarians expressed in Canadian dollars.
   Excludes medical and law libraries. See Tables 39 and 46 for salaries in medical and law libraries.

TABLE 18: NUMBER AND AVERAGE YEARS OF EXPERIENCE
OF ARL UNIVERSITY LIBRARIANS
BY POSITION AND SEX, FY 2005-06*

Position	Women		Men		Total	
	Years	No.	Years	No.	Years	No.
Director	31.1	63	31.6	49	31.3	112
Associate Director	25.8	150	23.8	100	25.0	250
Assistant Director	24.1	100	23.3	91	23.7	191
Head, Branch	22.0	357	22.2	174	22.1	531
Functional Specialist	13.4	929	12.6	760	13.0	1,689
Subject Specialist	17.6	589	17.2	386	17.4	975
Dept. Head: Acquisitions	22.0	77	24.1	29	22.6	106
Reference	22.3	87	19.2	38	21.3	125
Cataloging	22.4	139	21.7	52	22.2	191
Serials	19.1	30	23.8	8	20.1	38
Documents/Maps	19.5	57	20.8	32	20.0	89
Circulation	19.1	72	12.9	29	17.3	101
Rare Books/Manuscripts	21.7	36	24.1	46	23.0	82
Computer Systems	19.4	32	18.4	52	18.8	84
Other	19.1	393	19.7	243	19.3	636
Public Services	13.8	143	13.0	64	13.5	207
Technical Services	14.1	129	14.8	52	14.3	181
Administrative Services	14.9	121	14.3	43	14.8	164
Reference	14.3	1,056	15.1	436	14.5	1,492
Cataloger	17.6	500	16.9	251	17.4	751
All Positions	**17.2**	**5,061**	**17.0**	**2,935**	**17.1**	**7,996**

* Includes Canadian libraries. See Table 33 for comparable figures in Canadian libraries only.
   Excludes medical and law libraries. See Tables 40 and 47 for comparable figures in medical and law libraries.

TABLE 19: NUMBER AND AVERAGE SALARIES OF ARL UNIVERSITY LIBRARIANS BY YEARS OF EXPERIENCE AND SEX, FY 2005-06*

Experience	Women		Men		Total		% of Total
	Salary	No.	Salary	No.	Salary	No.	
0 - 3 years	$42,855	548	$46,177	305	$44,043	853	11%
4 - 7 years	48,125	731	51,010	469	49,253	1,200	15%
8 - 11 years	53,128	594	56,100	347	54,224	941	12%
12 - 15 years	58,302	550	60,258	310	59,007	860	11%
16 - 19 years	62,454	525	64,860	314	63,355	839	10%
20 - 23 years	66,445	527	70,085	261	67,650	788	10%
24 - 27 years	71,874	503	73,497	290	72,468	793	10%
28 - 31 years	74,643	453	78,187	304	76,066	757	9%
32 - 35 years	77,043	366	80,625	203	78,321	569	7%
over 35 years	79,112	264	87,358	132	81,861	396	5%
All Positions	**$61,083**	**5,061**	**$63,984**	**2,935**	**$62,148**	**7,996**	**100%**

* Canadian salaries expressed in U.S. dollars. See Table 34 for salaries in Canadian dollars.
   Excludes medical and law libraries. See Tables 41 and 48 for salaries in medical and law libraries.

TABLE 20: AVERAGE SALARIES OF ARL UNIVERSITY LIBRARIANS BY POSITION AND YEARS OF EXPERIENCE, FY 2005-06*

Years of Experience

Position	0–3 years	4–7 years	8–11 years	12–15 years	16–19 years	20–23 years	24–27 years	28–31 years	32–35 years	over 35 years
Director	N/A	N/A	N/A	N/A	†	$158,593	$160,041	$174,600	$173,538	$166,466
Associate Director	†	$77,968	$87,203	$96,464	$98,790	99,726	105,148	108,407	108,908	101,176
Assistant Director	$87,615	73,613	66,552	90,614	89,257	91,703	93,425	94,613	95,832	111,546
Head, Branch	48,326	50,793	59,539	63,140	67,721	69,829	71,814	78,613	79,092	86,669
Functional Specialist	44,817	50,153	55,246	57,797	60,752	66,959	66,133	70,121	70,668	70,420
Subject Specialist	44,708	49,163	53,630	57,412	61,645	60,497	66,892	66,557	70,873	71,198
Dept. Head: Acquisitions	†	53,155	61,454	61,693	65,096	73,415	66,161	72,777	76,517	75,676
Reference	†	49,555	61,130	65,471	67,078	71,936	77,914	75,742	77,912	67,970
Cataloging	†	49,426	56,242	59,485	65,762	67,840	67,743	73,076	72,713	69,408
Serials	†	48,440	†	60,885	66,767	60,759	68,312	†	67,858	†
Documents/Maps	43,257	50,430	52,258	55,565	56,855	63,732	66,409	67,436	75,158	67,867
Circulation	44,675	50,867	56,522	63,762	67,089	58,133	71,461	71,297	73,278	†
Rare Books/Manuscripts	†	68,138	58,096	65,595	65,795	77,992	76,761	78,338	79,928	90,526
Computer Systems	†	75,716	73,212	80,543	80,113	73,632	82,943	84,861	†	†
Other	51,740	53,899	59,305	64,875	65,191	69,187	72,731	73,551	74,583	78,333
Public Services	39,731	44,458	46,421	50,854	58,259	58,005	61,810	61,113	63,710	73,862
Technical Services	40,946	48,246	48,216	58,772	59,815	59,615	62,267	62,418	55,564	65,556
Administrative Services	47,180	52,165	50,719	62,990	61,076	63,291	59,788	70,422	†	102,895
Reference	41,086	46,363	49,686	52,484	55,609	57,753	61,132	61,181	61,727	64,319
Cataloger	43,355	46,097	47,823	51,336	55,520	57,549	57,082	57,207	60,888	62,342
All Positions: Average Salary	**$44,043**	**$49,253**	**$54,224**	**$59,007**	**$63,355**	**$67,650**	**$72,468**	**$76,066**	**$78,321**	**$81,861**
No. of Positions	**853**	**1,200**	**941**	**860**	**839**	**788**	**793**	**757**	**569**	**396**

* Years of experience reflect total professional experience. Canadian salaries expressed in U.S. dollars. Excludes medical and law libraries.
N/A - No positions reported in this category.
† Salary data are not published when fewer than four individuals are involved.

TABLE 21: NUMBER AND AVERAGE SALARIES OF ARL UNIVERSITY LIBRARIANS
BY POSITION AND TYPE OF INSTITUTION, FY 2005-06*

Position	Canadian (14) Salary	No.	Private (31) Salary	No.	Public (68) Salary	No.	Total (113) Salary	No.
Director	$115,721	14	$205,029	31	$163,286	67	$168,894	112
Associate Director	85,136	32	113,312	74	100,775	144	102,484	250
Assistant Director	73,124	15	100,118	70	90,171	106	92,478	191
Head, Branch	68,782	58	75,306	148	68,093	325	70,179	531
Functional Specialist	54,276	124	61,004	579	54,120	986	56,491	1,689
Subject Specialist	55,502	81	59,498	362	58,957	532	58,871	975
Dept. Head: Acquisitions	63,445	12	68,903	39	68,009	55	67,821	106
Reference	62,564	14	72,595	49	68,858	62	69,618	125
Cataloging	64,867	15	67,974	80	64,330	96	65,898	191
Serials	69,996	4	60,406	11	61,869	23	62,301	38
Documents/Maps	68,909	8	61,287	23	58,387	58	60,082	89
Circulation	59,482	14	58,395	34	63,723	53	61,342	101
Rare Books/Manuscripts	66,107	7	75,129	26	75,174	49	74,386	82
Computer Systems	66,877	9	82,614	32	79,497	43	79,332	84
Other	62,814	56	67,091	202	66,948	378	66,629	636
Reference: Over 14 years experience	62,447	108	58,437	169	58,496	376	59,134	653
10 to 14 years experience	54,000	31	53,394	50	50,066	139	51,377	220
5 to 9 years experience	48,224	47	49,559	79	46,500	170	47,591	296
Under 5 years experience	41,026	64	45,961	49	41,326	210	41,970	323
Cataloging: Over 14 years experience	60,009	46	58,984	160	56,130	217	57,631	423
10 to 14 years experience	45,895	6	50,742	39	48,956	54	49,474	99
5 to 9 years experience	45,227	6	49,509	51	45,487	53	47,338	110
Under 5 years experience	44,661	9	44,964	48	42,082	62	43,440	119
Other: Over 14 years experience	61,499	16	63,774	89	62,769	133	63,060	238
10 to 14 years experience	55,061	6	55,892	25	52,485	38	53,943	69
5 to 9 years experience	45,286	10	49,467	43	46,235	67	47,314	120
Under 5 years experience	40,222	12	47,940	41	41,730	72	43,622	125
All Positions	**$59,202**	**824**	**$65,165**	**2,603**	**$60,961**	**4,569**	**$62,148**	**7,996**

* Canadian salaries expressed in U.S. dollars. Tables 31-34 show Canadian salaries in Canadian dollars. Excludes medical and law libraries.
( ) Indicates the number of ARL libraries in each category.
‡ Salary data are not published when fewer than four individuals are involved.

TABLE 22: YEARS OF EXPERIENCE OF ARL UNIVERSITY LIBRARIANS BY POSITION AND TYPE OF INSTITUTION, FY 2005-06*

Position	Canadian (14) Years	No.	Private (31) Years	No.	Public (68) Years	No.	Total (113) Years	No.
Director	30.9	14	31.7	31	31.3	67	31.3	112
Associate Director	23.0	32	26.1	74	24.8	144	25.0	250
Assistant Director	23.9	15	24.4	70	23.2	106	23.7	191
Head, Branch	22.2	58	22.2	148	22.0	325	22.1	531
Functional Specialist	14.6	124	13.4	579	12.6	986	13.0	1,689
Subject Specialist	17.7	81	17.0	362	17.7	532	17.4	975
Dept. Head: Acquisitions	23.3	12	22.7	39	22.3	55	22.6	106
Reference	17.1	14	23.0	49	21.0	62	21.3	125
Cataloging	23.3	15	21.9	80	22.3	96	22.2	191
Serials	22.5	4	20.6	11	19.4	23	20.1	38
Documents/Maps	22.9	8	20.3	23	19.5	58	20.0	89
Circulation	19.1	14	16.4	34	17.4	53	17.3	101
Rare Books/Manuscripts	26.0	7	20.6	26	23.9	49	23.0	82
Computer Systems	23.0	9	18.2	32	18.3	43	18.8	84
Other	18.4	56	19.7	202	19.3	378	19.3	636
Reference: Over 14 years experience	24.9	108	25.1	169	24.7	376	24.8	653
10 to 14 years experience	11.8	31	12.0	50	11.9	139	11.9	220
5 to 9 years experience	6.3	47	6.7	79	6.8	170	6.7	296
Under 5 years experience	2.2	64	2.9	49	2.4	210	2.4	323
Cataloging: Over 14 years experience	26.8	46	25.2	160	25.8	217	25.7	423
10 to 14 years experience	11.5	6	12.2	39	11.9	54	12.0	99
5 to 9 years experience	6.8	6	6.6	51	6.7	53	6.7	110
Under 5 years experience	2.4	9	2.5	48	2.4	62	2.4	119
Other: Over 14 years experience	25.3	16	24.1	89	25.4	133	24.9	238
10 to 14 years experience	12.3	6	11.6	25	11.7	38	11.7	69
5 to 9 years experience	6.4	10	6.7	43	6.5	67	6.6	120
Under 5 years experience	2.2	12	2.7	41	2.2	72	2.3	125
All Positions	**17.4**	**824**	**17.4**	**2,603**	**16.9**	**4,569**	**17.1**	**7,996**

* Excludes medical and law libraries.
( ) Indicates the number of ARL libraries in each category.

TABLE 23: NUMBER AND AVERAGE SALARIES OF ARL UNIVERSITY LIBRARIANS BY POSITION AND SIZE OF PROFESSIONAL STAFF, FY 2005-06*

Position	Staff Over 110 (10) ‡ Salary	No.	Staff 75-110 (23) Salary	No.	Staff 50-74 (43) Salary	No.	Staff 21-49 (37) § Salary	No.
Director	$208,691	10	$183,967	22	$163,679	43	$155,238	37
Associate Director	117,133	48	111,582	53	95,513	76	93,503	73
Assistant Director	93,968	29	98,745	50	89,949	81	87,583	31
Head, Branch	77,124	132	72,310	137	65,262	164	66,071	98
Functional Specialist	61,647	436	57,457	491	53,388	528	51,861	234
Subject Specialist	62,924	245	60,412	268	55,862	343	55,730	119
Dept. Head: Acquisitions	72,296	18	74,079	22	63,980	32	65,019	34
Reference	77,538	21	73,876	26	63,682	43	68,995	35
Cataloging	72,891	48	68,871	48	58,744	54	63,654	41
Serials	65,840	5	64,773	8	59,035	16	63,943	9
Documents/Maps	70,720	12	64,051	22	56,709	32	55,429	23
Circulation	65,728	15	60,256	31	58,210	35	65,215	20
Rare Books/Manuscripts	90,877	7	81,384	18	69,352	28	70,921	29
Computer Systems	102,333	7	81,554	23	77,246	30	73,101	24
Other	71,552	108	71,448	182	61,430	224	64,629	122
Reference: Over 14 years experience	63,559	94	59,014	187	58,305	194	57,827	178
10 to 14 years experience	54,258	34	51,181	60	50,598	70	50,809	56
5 to 9 years experience	50,299	58	47,307	70	47,590	100	45,574	68
Under 5 years experience	44,993	38	43,163	91	40,791	114	40,855	80
Cataloging: Over 14 years experience	63,570	108	57,159	119	53,266	138	57,927	58
10 to 14 years experience	52,464	17	50,836	36	46,694	27	48,168	19
5 to 9 years experience	51,107	38	46,316	29	43,809	31	46,987	12
Under 5 years experience	47,110	36	42,690	20	41,857	36	41,213	27
Other: Over 14 years experience	65,709	60	62,798	66	60,114	82	66,389	30
10 to 14 years experience	56,327	16	53,973	21	50,893	19	55,419	13
5 to 9 years experience	50,151	40	45,580	33	44,808	33	49,206	14
Under 5 years experience	48,281	34	42,093	40	39,615	27	44,078	24
All Positions	**$65,878**	**1,714**	**$62,974**	**2,173**	**$59,459**	**2,600**	**$61,355**	**1,509**

*Canadian salaries expressed in U.S. dollars. For average Canadian salaries (expressed in U.S. dollars) refer to Table 21; Tables 31-34 show Canadian salaries in Canadian dollars. Excludes medical and law libraries.

( ) Indicates the number of ARL libraries in each category.

‡ In 1995-96 and earlier, the first column of this table reported staff over 124; in 1996-98 over 120; in 1998-99 over 115; and since 1999-2000, over 110.

§ No ARL Library has fewer than 21 professional staff members.

TABLE 24: YEARS OF EXPERIENCE OF ARL UNIVERSITY LIBRARIANS
BY POSITION AND SIZE OF PROFESSIONAL STAFF, FY 2005-06*

Position	Staff Over 110 (10)†		Staff 75-110 (23)		Staff 50-74 (43)		Staff 24-49 (37)‡	
	Years	No.	Years	No.	Years	No.	Years	No.
Director	31.8	10	31.4	22	31.5	43	30.9	37
Associate Director	25.5	48	24.5	53	24.4	76	25.6	73
Assistant Director	22.3	29	23.8	50	23.1	81	26.4	31
Head, Branch	22.3	132	22.5	137	20.9	164	23.2	98
Functional Specialist	12.9	436	13.4	491	12.6	528	13.4	234
Subject Specialist	16.8	245	17.2	268	18.0	343	17.9	119
Dept. Head: Acquisitions	24.8	18	22.9	22	20.5	32	23.1	34
Reference	22.9	21	21.1	26	20.6	43	21.5	35
Cataloging	22.3	48	23.1	48	21.2	54	22.5	41
Serials	15.4	5	24.3	8	18.2	16	22.3	9
Documents/Maps	24.0	12	22.8	22	19.3	32	16.2	23
Circulation	19.5	15	14.8	31	16.8	35	20.4	20
Rare Books/Manuscripts	24.9	7	23.3	18	24.7	28	20.8	29
Computer Systems	25.0	7	18.4	23	17.1	30	19.4	24
Other	20.1	108	20.5	182	17.8	224	19.5	122
Reference: Over 14 years experience	25.1	94	25.5	187	24.4	194	24.5	178
10 to 14 years experience	12.0	34	11.8	60	11.9	70	12.1	56
5 to 9 years experience	6.5	58	6.7	70	6.8	100	6.8	68
Under 5 years experience	2.7	38	2.4	91	2.4	114	2.3	80
Cataloging: Over 14 years experience	25.9	108	25.2	119	26.4	138	24.6	58
10 to 14 years experience	12.1	17	11.9	36	11.9	27	12.1	19
5 to 9 years experience	6.4	38	6.7	29	6.8	31	7.0	12
Under 5 years experience	2.3	36	2.2	20	2.4	36	2.9	27
Other: Over 14 years experience	25.6	60	24.4	66	25.3	82	23.6	30
10 to 14 years experience	11.6	16	11.2	21	11.9	19	12.4	13
5 to 9 years experience	6.5	40	6.4	33	6.8	33	6.8	14
Under 5 years experience	2.2	34	2.4	40	2.4	27	2.5	24
All Positions	**16.7**	**1,714**	**17.2**	**2,173**	**16.9**	**2,600**	**17.8**	**1,509**

* Excludes medical and law libraries.

( ) Indicates the number of ARL libraries in each category.

† In 1995-96 and earlier, the first column of this table reported staff over 124; in 1996-98, over 120; in 1998-99, over 115; and since 1999-2000, over 110.

‡ No ARL library has fewer than 21 professional staff members.

TABLE 25: AVERAGE SALARIES OF ARL UNIVERSITY LIBRARIANS BY POSITION AND GEOGRAPHIC REGION, FY 2005–06*

Position	Northeast New England (9)	Northeast Middle Atlantic (14)	North Central East N.Central (17)	North Central West N.Central (7)	South South Atlantic (18)	South East S.Central (6)	South West S.Central (9)	West Mountain (7)	West Pacific (12)	Canada (14)	Total (113)
Director	$180,846	$210,114	$168,257	$164,604	$182,260	$151,086	$175,438	$147,808	$173,477	$115,721	$168,894
Associate Director	122,836	115,114	100,974	101,747	100,078	87,233	94,653	98,738	110,927	85,136	102,484
Assistant Director	89,772	98,539	88,307	93,519	89,592	†	87,741	96,246	118,271	73,124	92,478
Head, Branch	81,640	76,036	69,672	66,707	61,127	62,373	63,369	69,204	73,251	68,782	70,179
Functional Specialist	63,055	58,622	50,777	57,098	56,013	50,985	48,702	55,124	64,485	54,276	56,491
Subject Specialist	63,595	61,218	57,392	58,062	52,870	48,387	51,340	58,805	66,252	55,502	58,871
Dept. Head: Acquisitions	72,603	66,823	67,516	67,618	68,160	75,757	58,508	74,890	64,269	63,445	67,821
Reference	74,769	76,621	67,506	69,301	68,884	66,791	57,432	66,405	81,652	62,564	69,618
Cataloging	76,694	64,957	63,776	62,116	58,839	58,244	62,053	71,912	68,556	64,867	65,898
Serials	†	69,038	62,187	†	57,715	†	†	61,589	65,029	69,996	62,301
Documents/Maps	64,640	62,023	56,418	61,253	57,157	†	55,404	50,851	68,247	68,909	60,082
Circulation	63,800	59,997	63,938	63,381	62,228	†	54,833	71,549	61,196	59,482	61,342
Rare Books/Manuscripts	87,249	77,713	67,930	80,319	74,674	†	55,510	68,267	81,430	66,107	74,386
Computer Systems	87,453	89,646	76,661	78,917	75,050	77,300	77,564	81,653	82,896	66,877	79,332
Other	74,202	68,575	66,586	64,018	65,693	64,100	57,744	65,851	74,348	62,814	66,629
Reference: Over 14 years experience	64,757	59,882	57,181	53,724	53,705	58,044	46,805	56,449	65,875	62,447	59,134
10 to 14 years experience	56,358	51,130	49,363	47,073	49,756	48,927	45,858	50,531	55,223	54,000	51,377
5 to 9 years experience	52,438	47,439	46,838	46,660	46,381	44,539	41,132	46,541	48,970	48,224	47,591
Under 5 years experience	49,380	43,254	42,407	43,319	42,057	42,348	37,859	40,033	42,690	41,026	41,970
Cataloging: Over 14 years experience	63,135	58,202	54,445	54,970	53,426	51,396	47,030	55,351	65,998	60,009	57,631
10 to 14 years experience	54,222	50,369	50,407	46,183	46,087	†	44,976	50,478	53,697	45,895	49,474
5 to 9 years experience	52,780	45,452	46,689	45,006	44,539	†	42,108	45,020	50,824	45,227	47,338
Under 5 years experience	47,778	44,178	41,662	40,891	42,210	40,103	38,475	42,376	45,274	44,661	43,440
Other: Over 14 years experience	66,767	63,698	65,740	53,013	58,823	61,472	52,676	56,567	68,164	61,499	63,060
10 to 14 years experience	57,300	54,524	53,982	53,574	48,250	†	51,603	51,571	†	55,061	53,943
5 to 9 years experience	52,918	51,976	45,782	44,694	45,463	45,782	41,287	41,230	49,271	45,286	47,314
Under 5 years experience	50,148	38,698	40,097	47,337	42,659	43,305	40,198	46,850	48,248	40,222	43,622
All Positions: Average Salary	**$66,944**	**$64,942**	**$59,959**	**$60,437**	**$60,293**	**$58,060**	**$55,267**	**$60,780**	**$68,789**	**$59,202**	**$62,148**
No. of Staff	**1,085**	**1,097**	**1,286**	**435**	**1,123**	**304**	**581**	**416**	**845**	**824**	**7,996**

* Canadian salaries expressed in U.S. dollars. Excludes medical and law libraries.

( ) Indicates number of ARL libraries included.

† Salary data are not published when fewer than four individuals are involved.

N/A – No positions were reported in this category.

ARL UNIVERSITY LIBRARIES BY GEOGRAPHIC REGION*

Region	No. of Libs.	ARL University Libraries Included	States/Provinces Included
Northeast			
1. New England	(9)	Boston University, Boston College, Brown, Connecticut, Dartmouth, Harvard, Massachusetts Institute of Technology, Massachusetts, Yale	Conn., Mass., Me., N.H., R.I., Vt.
2. Middle Atlantic	(14)	Columbia; Cornell; New York; Pennsylvania; Pennsylvania State; Pittsburgh; Princeton; Rochester; Rutgers; State University of New York: Albany, Buffalo, Stony Brook; Syracuse; Temple	N.J., N.Y., Pa.
North Central			
3. East North Central	(17)	Case Western Reserve, Chicago, Cincinnati, Illinois-Chicago, Illinois-Urbana, Indiana, Kent State, Michigan, Michigan State, Notre Dame, Northwestern, Ohio University, Ohio State, Purdue, Southern Illinois, Wayne State, Wisconsin	Ill., Ind., Mich., Ohio, Wis.
4. West North Central	(7)	Iowa, Iowa State, Kansas, Minnesota, Missouri, Nebraska, Washington U.-St. Louis	Iowa, Kan., Minn., Mo., Neb., N. Dak., S. Dak.
South			
5. South Atlantic	(18)	Delaware, Duke, Emory, Florida, Florida State, Georgia, Georgia Tech., Georgetown, George Washington, Howard, Johns Hopkins, Maryland, Miami, North Carolina, North Carolina State, South Carolina, Virginia, Virginia Tech	Del., D.C., Fla., Ga., Md., N.C., S.C., Va., W. Va.
6. East South Central	(6)	Alabama, Auburn, Kentucky, Louisville, Tennessee, Vanderbilt	Ala., Ky., Miss., Tenn.
7. West South Central	(9)	Houston, Louisiana State, Oklahoma, Oklahoma State, Rice, Texas, Texas A&M, Texas Tech, Tulane	Ark., La., Okla., Tex.
West			
8. Mountain	(7)	Arizona, Arizona State, Brigham Young, Colorado, Colorado State, New Mexico, Utah	Ariz., Colo., Idaho, Mont., Nev., N. Mex., Utah, Wyo.
9. Pacific	(13)	University of California: Berkeley, Davis, Irvine, Los Angeles, Riverside, San Diego, Santa Barbara; Hawaii; Oregon; Southern California; Washington; Washington State	Alaska, Calif., Hawaii, Ore., Wash.
Canada	(14)	Alberta, British Columbia, Guelph, Laval, McGill, McMaster, Manitoba, Montreal, Queen's, Saskatchewan, Toronto, Waterloo, Western Ontario, York	Alta., B.C., Man., N. Br., Newf., N.S., Ont., P.E.I., Que., Sask.

*Regions are based on the classification used by the U. S. Bureau of the Census in tabulations of the Current Population Survey.

\

U.S. ARL UNIVERSITY LIBRARIES

Tables 26–30

TABLE 26: AVERAGE SALARIES OF U.S. ARL UNIVERSITY LIBRARIANS BY POSITION AND YEARS OF EXPERIENCE, FY 2005-06*

Position	Years of Experience									
	0 - 3	4 - 7	8 - 11	12-15	16-19	20-23	24-27	28-31	32-35	Over 35
Director	N/A	N/A	N/A	N/A	†	177,465	168,262	178,566	180,739	174,755
Associate Director	†	81,227	89,274	100,744	98,791	103,402	108,842	109,774	111,956	101,479
Assistant Director	87,615	73,613	69,488	93,847	90,732	91,703	94,434	94,991	102,028	115,440
Head, Branch	49,026	49,679	59,753	63,429	67,902	69,505	72,392	79,096	79,315	86,535
Functional Specialist	45,000	50,537	55,472	57,839	61,224	67,516	65,991	71,536	70,811	69,351
Subject Specialist	45,443	49,610	53,944	57,727	61,403	60,054	67,683	67,104	71,639	71,348
Dept. Head: Acquisitions	†	53,155	63,524	61,693	66,596	73,279	66,826	74,565	76,876	75,631
Reference	N/A	49,612	63,629	66,433	67,351	72,781	78,052	75,812	77,698	67,970
Cataloging	†	49,968	56,242	59,477	65,667	67,990	68,123	72,649	72,713	70,178
Serials	†	48,440	†	60,885	†	60,759	66,236	†	67,858	†
Documents/Maps	43,257	48,924	52,258	54,429	55,646	63,077	66,409	67,571	75,158	64,394
Circulation	44,675	52,182	56,549	66,343	65,205	58,108	70,714	73,296	76,601	†
Rare Books/Manuscripts	†	68,138	58,096	65,595	66,915	77,992	78,617	78,559	82,919	90,526
Computer Systems	†	75,716	75,311	80,543	80,574	79,609	82,943	86,813	†	†
Other	52,448	54,693	59,343	65,241	65,240	69,687	73,005	74,271	74,926	77,840
Public Services	39,608	44,760	46,644	50,427	58,852	55,915	61,810	61,113	63,710	73,862
Technical Services	40,961	48,637	47,752	58,772	59,815	59,837	61,877	62,948	56,187	65,705
Administrative Services	48,088	51,927	51,812	62,967	61,635	66,321	60,895	70,422	†	100,204
Reference	41,170	46,493	49,105	52,382	54,423	56,564	60,714	61,704	60,285	63,345
Cataloger	43,200	46,120	48,282	51,512	55,692	57,728	56,656	56,219	60,663	61,528
All Positions										
Average Salary	**$44,425**	**$49,588**	**$54,416**	**$59,143**	**$63,386**	**$67,771**	**$72,844**	**$77,440**	**$79,073**	**$82,076**
Number of Staff	**758**	**1,075**	**870**	**775**	**738**	**715**	**710**	**670**	**504**	**357**

* Excludes Canadian libraries. Excludes medical and law libraries.
† Salary data are not published when fewer than four individuals are involved.
N/A - No positions were reported in this category.

TABLE 27: NUMBER AND AVERAGE SALARIES OF MINORITY U.S. ARL UNIVERSITY LIBRARIANS BY POSITION AND SEX, FY 2005-06*

Position	Women Salary	Women No.	Men Salary	Men No.	Total Salary	Total No.
Director	†	3	†	2	155,233	5
Associate Director	†	13	†	2	103,174	15
Assistant Director	97,722	4	91,883	4	94,802	8
Head, Branch	63,183	39	80,284	10	66,673	49
Functional Specialist	51,865	126	55,488	79	53,261	205
Subject Specialist	56,510	121	57,550	58	56,847	179
Dept. Head: Acquisitions	†	6	†	1	65,872	7
Reference	†	6	†	3	64,906	9
Cataloging	67,166	12	65,511	6	66,615	18
Serials	†	2	N/A		†	2
Documents/Maps	†	7	†	1	52,114	8
Circulation	47,855	5	61,526	6	55,312	11
Rare Books/Manuscripts	65,868	4	N/A		65,868	4
Computer Systems	†	3	†	7	76,028	10
Other	66,080	42	69,662	16	67,068	58
Reference: Over 14 years experience	58,705	58	59,956	15	58,962	73
10 to 14 years experience	51,306	18	49,736	7	50,866	25
5 to 9 years experience	48,367	20	47,389	11	48,020	31
Under 5 years experience	41,789	36	43,035	10	42,060	46
Cataloging: Over 14 years experience	55,928	37	59,449	14	56,895	51
10 to 14 years experience	49,539	14	47,844	4	49,162	18
5 to 9 years experience	50,816	16	45,734	6	49,430	22
Under 5 years experience	41,381	13	43,486	10	42,296	23
Other: Over 14 years experience	†	9	†	1	73,210	10
10 to 14 years experience	†	6	†	1	51,925	7
5 to 9 years experience	†	8	†	2	51,887	10
Under 5 years experience	†	13	†	2	43,105	15
All Positions	**$56,957**	**641**	**$58,711**	**278**	**$57,488**	**919**

* Excludes Canadian libraries. Excludes medical and law libraries.
† Salary data are not published when fewer than four individuals are involved in either category.
N/A - No positions were reported in this category.

TABLE 28: NUMBER AND AVERAGE YEARS OF EXPERIENCE OF MINORITY U.S. ARL UNIVERSITY LIBRARIANS BY POSITION AND SEX, FY 2005-06*

Position	Women		Men		Total	
	Years	No.	Years	No.	Years	No.
Director	32.0	3	38.0	2	34.4	5
Associate Director	25.0	13	27.5	2	25.3	15
Assistant Director	24.5	4	19.3	4	21.9	8
Head, Branch	22.8	39	21.7	10	22.6	49
Functional Specialist	11.0	126	10.8	79	10.9	205
Subject Specialist	14.5	121	12.8	58	13.9	179
Dept. Head: Acquisitions	22.8	6	35.0	1	24.6	7
Reference	21.2	6	18.3	3	20.2	9
Cataloging	18.8	12	23.2	6	20.2	18
Serials	7.5	2	N/A		7.5	2
Documents/Maps	9.0	7	8.0	1	8.9	8
Circulation	19.6	5	11.7	6	15.3	11
Rare Books/Manuscripts	13.3	4	N/A		13.3	4
Computer Systems	18.7	3	16.9	7	17.4	10
Other	17.5	42	19.3	16	18.0	58
Public Services	7.0	14	13.7	3	8.2	17
Technical Services	12.3	12	6.5	2	11.4	14
Administrative Services	11.8	10	1.0	1	10.8	11
Reference	13.7	132	13.0	43	13.5	175
Cataloger	16.0	80	13.8	34	15.3	114
All Positions	**14.8**	**641**	**13.8**	**278**	**14.5**	**919**

*Excludes Canadian libraries. Excludes medical and law libraries.
N/A - No positions were reported in this category.

TABLE 29: NUMBER AND AVERAGE SALARIES OF
U.S. ARL UNIVERSITY LIBRARIANS
BY YEARS OF EXPERIENCE AND SEX, FY 2005-06*

| Experience | Women | | Men | | Total | | % of |
	Salary	No.	Salary	No.	Salary	No.	Total
0 - 3 years	$43,088	483	$46,772	275	$44,425	758	11%
4 - 7 years	48,399	645	51,372	430	49,588	1,075	15%
8 - 11 years	53,269	550	56,389	320	54,416	870	12%
12 - 15 years	58,466	491	60,315	284	59,143	775	11%
16 - 19 years	62,486	458	64,859	280	63,386	738	10%
20 - 23 years	66,278	476	70,746	239	67,771	715	10%
24 - 27 years	72,048	450	74,222	260	72,844	710	10%
28 - 31 years	76,091	394	79,365	276	77,440	670	9%
32 - 35 years	77,626	325	81,702	179	79,073	504	7%
over 35 years	78,743	236	88,576	121	82,076	357	5%
All Positions	**$61,316**	**4,508**	**$64,467**	**2,664**	**$62,487**	**7,172**	**100%**

*Excludes Canadian libraries. Excludes medical and law libraries.

TABLE 30: NUMBER AND AVERAGE SALARIES OF MINORITY
U.S. ARL UNIVERSITY LIBRARIANS
BY YEARS OF EXPERIENCE AND SEX, FY 2005-06*

| Experience | Women | | Men | | Total | | % of |
	Salary	No.	Salary	No.	Salary	No.	Total
0 - 3 years	$42,515	107	$44,541	36	$43,025	143	16%
4 - 7 years	48,550	93	50,734	76	49,532	169	18%
8 - 11 years	52,817	89	56,424	41	53,955	130	14%
12 - 15 years	58,178	84	61,458	28	58,998	112	12%
16 - 19 years	61,976	72	67,203	24	63,283	96	10%
20 - 23 years	60,770	54	60,994	10	60,805	64	7%
24 - 27 years	65,418	39	70,270	20	67,063	59	6%
28 - 31 years	73,829	44	67,401	14	72,277	58	6%
32 - 35 years	76,247	32	75,552	15	76,025	47	5%
over 35 years	69,402	27	80,222	14	73,097	41	4%
All Positions	**$56,957**	**641**	**$58,711**	**278**	**$57,488**	**919**	**100%**

*Excludes Canadian libraries. Excludes medical and law libraries.

CANADIAN ARL UNIVERSITY LIBRARIES

Tables 31–34

TABLE 31: FILLED POSITIONS; AVERAGE, MEDIAN, AND BEGINNING PROFESSIONAL SALARIES; AND AVERAGE YEARS OF PROFESSIONAL EXPERIENCE IN CANADIAN ARL UNIVERSITY LIBRARIES, FY 2005-06*

Institution	Filled Positions FY 2006	Average Salaries		Median Salaries		Beginning Salaries		Average Yrs. Exp. FY 2006
		FY 2005	FY 2006	FY2005	FY2006	FY2005	FY2006	
Alberta ‡	65	$78,706	$79,028	$82,364	$84,550	$43,910	$45,447	16.9
British Columbia ‡	76	73,931	71,766	72,085	68,910	44,700	44,700	16.1
Guelph ‡	39	67,991	71,439	65,278	69,447	41,187	42,217	18.6
Laval	63	65,415	62,559	69,620	68,283	42,683	42,683	17.6
McGill ‡	55	69,949	70,820	73,414	73,217	41,000	41,000	19.6
McMaster ‡	25	69,692	69,652	68,190	69,384	39,610	40,798	18.5
Manitoba ‡	43	76,794	79,885	80,379	82,526	42,566	43,843	22.9
Montreal ‡	90	63,666	63,733	63,214	63,214	40,260	41,541	16.1
Queen's ‡	34	73,795	76,676	73,355	76,660	42,149	43,413	19.3
Saskatchewan ‡	38	74,423	73,473	72,008	70,212	41,807	41,807	16.8
Toronto ‡	144	77,937	79,101	82,426	81,799	45,000	45,800	16.8
Waterloo ‡	33	70,159	72,667	71,212	74,767	40,517	41,854	20.0
Western Ontario ‡	64	59,280	60,795	56,795	58,057	45,340	46,470	14.2
York ‡	55	84,327	86,418	82,738	80,371	42,226	42,225	16.4

* Salaries expressed in Canadian dollars. Directors are included in figures for average years of experience and filled positions, but not in the average and median salary statistics. Excludes Canadian medical and law libraries. See Tables 35 and 42 for statistics related to medical and law library salaries.

‡ See Footnotes.

TABLE 32: NUMBER AND AVERAGE SALARIES OF
CANADIAN ARL UNIVERSITY LIBRARIANS
BY POSITION AND SEX, FY 2005-06*

Position	Women Salary	No.	Men Salary	No.	Total Salary	No.
Director	$151,078	7	$138,159	7	$144,618	14
Associate Director	104,005	22	111,653	10	106,395	32
Assistant Director	91,314	7	91,444	8	91,384	15
Head, Branch	86,425	42	84,730	16	85,957	58
Functional Specialist	69,128	59	66,651	65	67,829	124
Subject Specialist	69,433	50	69,245	31	69,361	81
Dept. Head: Acquisitions	†	9	†	3	79,288	12
Reference	†	12	†	2	78,187	14
Cataloging	†	13	†	2	81,065	15
Serials	87,474	4	N/A		87,474	4
Documents/Maps	†	6	†	2	86,116	8
Circulation	†	13	†	1	74,336	14
Rare Books/Manuscripts	†	3	†	4	82,615	7
Computer Systems	75,982	5	93,069	4	83,577	9
Other	78,939	36	77,705	20	78,499	56
Reference: Over 14 years experience	77,279	79	80,116	29	78,040	108
10 to 14 years experience	68,990	23	63,155	8	67,484	31
5 to 9 years experience	61,041	36	57,730	11	60,267	47
Under 5 years experience	51,262	51	51,306	13	51,271	64
Cataloging: Over 14 years experience	78,384	29	69,210	17	74,994	46
10 to 14 years experience	†	3	†	3	57,356	6
5 to 9 years experience	†	4	†	2	56,521	6
Under 5 years experience	†	7	†	2	55,813	9
Other: Over 14 years experience	†	13	†	3	76,856	16
10 to 14 years experience	†	4	†	2	68,810	6
5 to 9 years experience	†	9	†	1	56,595	10
Under 5 years experience	50,277	7	50,249	5	50,265	12
All Positions	**$73,962**	**553**	**$74,033**	**271**	**$73,985**	**824**

* Excludes Canadian medical and law libraries. See Tables 39 and 46 for salaries in medical and law libraries.
    Salaries expressed in Canadian dollars.
†Salary data are not published when fewer than four individuals are involved in either category.
N/A - No positions were reported in this category.

TABLE 33: NUMBER AND AVERAGE YEARS OF EXPERIENCE OF CANADIAN ARL UNIVERSITY LIBRARIANS BY POSITION AND SEX, FY 2005-06*

Position	Women Years	Women No.	Men Years	Men No.	Total Years	Total No.
Director	32.0	7	29.7	7	30.9	14
Associate Director	22.8	22	23.5	10	23.0	32
Assistant Director	22.7	7	25.0	8	23.9	15
Head, Branch	22.5	42	21.4	16	22.2	58
Functional Specialist	14.4	59	14.8	65	14.6	124
Subject Specialist	18.1	50	17.2	31	17.7	81
Dept. Head: Acquisitions	24.7	9	19.3	3	23.3	12
Reference	16.5	12	21.0	2	17.1	14
Cataloging	24.0	13	18.5	2	23.3	15
Serials	22.5	4	N/A		22.5	4
Documents/Maps	26.2	6	13.0	2	22.9	8
Circulation	19.5	13	15.0	1	19.1	14
Rare Books/Manuscripts	28.0	3	24.5	4	26.0	7
Computer Systems	22.6	5	23.5	4	23.0	9
Other	19.5	36	16.4	20	18.4	56
Public Services	9.6	10	7.4	5	8.9	15
Technical Services	15.2	10	13.0	3	14.7	13
Administrations	15.8	13	12.7	3	15.3	16
Reference	13.5	189	15.5	61	14.0	250
Cataloger	20.1	43	20.9	24	20.4	67
All Positions	**17.3**	**553**	**17.5**	**271**	**17.4**	**824**

* Excludes Canadian medical and law libraries. See Tables 40 and 47 for figures in medical and law libraries.
N/A - No positions were reported in this category.

TABLE 34: NUMBER AND AVERAGE SALARIES OF
CANADIAN ARL UNIVERSITY LIBRARIANS
BY YEARS OF EXPERIENCE AND SEX, FY 2005-06*

| Experience | Women | | Men | | Total | | % of |
	Salary	No.	Salary	No.	Salary	No.	Total
0 - 3 years	$51,389	65	$50,894	30	$51,233	95	12%
4 - 7 years	57,578	86	58,758	39	57,946	125	15%
8 - 11 years	64,198	44	65,836	27	64,821	71	9%
12 - 15 years	71,161	59	74,526	26	72,190	85	10%
16 - 19 years	77,774	67	81,067	34	78,883	101	12%
20 - 23 years	84,985	51	78,612	22	83,064	73	9%
24 - 27 years	87,971	53	83,999	30	86,536	83	10%
28 - 31 years	81,191	59	83,195	28	81,836	87	11%
32 - 35 years	90,507	41	90,727	24	90,588	65	8%
over 35 years	102,751	28	92,434	11	99,841	39	5%
All Positions	**$73,962**	**553**	**$74,033**	**271**	**$73,985**	**824**	**100%**

*Excludes Canadian medical and law libraries. See Tables 41 and 48 for salaries in medical and law libraries.
Salaries expressed in Canadian dollars.

ARL UNIVERSITY MEDICAL LIBRARIES

Tables 35–41

TABLE 35: FILLED POSITIONS; AVERAGE, MEDIAN, BEGINNING PROFESSIONAL SALARIES; AND AVERAGE YEARS OF PROFESSIONAL EXPERIENCE
ARL UNIVERSITY MEDICAL LIBRARIES, FY 2005-06*

Institution	Filled Positions	Average Salary	Median Salary	Beginning Salary	Average Yrs. Exp.
Alabama	3	‡	‡	35,000	16.3
Alberta	5	66,311	68,610	36,366	17.4
Arizona	16	58,226	53,398	41,688	21.3
Boston University	8	54,414	55,593	38,500	14.4
British Columbia	12	53,595	55,069	35,768	16.2
California, Davis	10	68,072	66,558	37,920	20.1
California, Irvine	2	‡	‡	37,920	15.5
California, Los Angeles	17	66,956	64,332	37,920	15.2
California, San Diego	9	69,644	60,100	37,920	16.3
Case Western Reserve	10	58,167	62,647	35,000	24.5
Cincinnati	20	61,046	56,757	35,000	23.2
Columbia	9	55,400	52,034	47,500	15.4
Connecticut	13	70,790	68,386	50,897	16.2
Cornell	9	69,764	69,443	45,000	18.2
Dartmouth	9	52,046	51,349	37,000	15.9
Duke	20	54,227	54,349	36,850	16.4
Emory	11	55,385	51,838	37,000	21.3
Florida	15	53,641	54,497	40,000	18.6
Florida State	3	‡	‡	34,000	18.7
George Washington	16	59,222	55,342	42,000	15.5
Georgetown	8	54,262	55,944	38,000	10.5
Harvard	22	65,437	62,009	43,000	11.5
Howard	7	50,145	47,769	35,049	20.6
Illinois, Chicago	20	57,895	52,994	40,000	15.3
Iowa	12	56,853	48,465	42,600	17.2
Johns Hopkins	28	62,208	55,221	32,800	14.1
Kansas	10	46,601	44,716	37,500	14.0
Kentucky	15	51,939	51,683	31,000	18.2
Louisiana State	2	‡	‡	36,000	20.0
Louisville	7	51,613	49,289	32,808	21.9
McGill	8	51,616	51,205	32,646	15.3
McMaster	11	52,546	48,783	35,083	19.9
Manitoba	14	50,152	46,576	38,000	12.9
Miami	11	59,807	57,960	40,000	22.5
Michigan	15	54,690	51,036	36,000	14.9
Minnesota	11	59,938	56,950	32,500	12.3
Missouri	9	42,498	41,484	38,771	13.2
Montreal	10	51,007	50,583	35,000	19.1
Nebraska	11	56,569	50,470	36,750	16.8

*Directors are included in figures for average years of experience and filled positions, but not in either the average or median salary statistics.

† Canadian salaries expressed in U.S. dollars.

‡ Salary data are not published when fewer than four individuals are involved.

§ See Footnotes.

TABLE 35: FILLED POSITIONS; AVERAGE, MEDIAN, BEGINNING PROFESSIONAL SALARIES; AND AVERAGE YEARS OF PROFESSIONAL EXPERIENCE
ARL UNIVERSITY MEDICAL LIBRARIES, FY 2005-06*

Institution	Filled Positions	Average Salary	Median Salary	Beginning Salary	Average Yrs. Exp.
New Mexico	19	73,591	65,279	45,000	17.2
New York University	24	65,936	62,412	48,500	16.2
North Carolina	30	56,808	56,734	38,000	19.2
Northwestern	13	55,919	58,856	40,000	16.7
Ohio State	11	58,112	56,968	30,000	13.7
Oklahoma	7	48,889	50,551	34,000	18.9
Oklahoma State	3	‡	‡	40,000	23.3
Pennsylvania	14	55,505	51,877	39,000	15.5
Pennsylvania State	5	54,072	50,364	39,000	18.4
Pittsburgh	27	52,648	48,885	34,738	14.2
Queen`s	7	50,766	49,317	36,000	13.6
Rochester	20	51,213	47,247	33,453	19.4
Saskatchewan	6	43,731	40,665	34,000	5.5
South Carolina	6	41,788	37,262	42,500	10.5
Southern California	14	68,518	69,071	35,000	18.6
Southern Illinois	6	52,609	54,624	38,753	20.5
SUNY Buffalo	15	55,304	53,760	40,000	16.7
SUNY Stony Brook	20	59,816	58,490	36,500	10.8
Temple	12	48,726	49,849	38,000	16.9
Tennessee, Knoxville	4	41,525	41,889	41,000	14.5
Tennessee, Memphis	13	52,526	48,543	40,000	22.5
Texas Tech	21	47,004	43,527	38,388	20.7
Toronto	17	66,310	72,063	36,649	15.7
Tulane	8	45,508	41,200	34,000	19.5
Utah	15	52,380	49,157	33,000	16.7
Vanderbilt	23	52,454	50,851	36,000	11.0
Virginia	15	56,036	58,400	45,000	15.8
Washington	20	57,618	53,640	38,800	20.0
Washington U.-St. Louis	22	57,283	46,996	38,000	23.2
Wayne State	12	43,963	40,918	40,000	9.8
Wisconsin	19	53,295	51,805	37,719	10.1
Yale	17	65,228	62,178	40,400	14.7

*Directors are included in figures for average years of experience and filled positions, but not in either the average or median salary statistics.
† Canadian salaries expressed in U.S. dollars.
‡ Salary data are not published when fewer than four individuals are involved.
§ See Footnotes.

TABLE 36: BEGINNING PROFESSIONAL SALARIES
IN ARL UNIVERSITY MEDICAL LIBRARIES
RANK ORDER TABLE, FY 2005-06*

Rank	Institution	Salary	Rank	Institution	Salary
1	Connecticut	$50,897	34	Calif. Davis	$37,920
2	North Carolina	48,500	38	Wisconsin	37,719
3	Columbia	47,500	39	Kentucky	37,500
4	Virginia	45,000	40	Emory	37,000
4	New York	45,000	40	Dartmouth	37,000
4	Cornell	45,000	42	Duke	36,850
7	Harvard	43,000	43	New Mexico	36,750
8	Johns Hopkins	42,600	44	Toronto	36,649
9	Southern California	42,500	45	Temple	36,500
10	George Washington	42,000	46	Alberta	36,366
11	Arizona	41,688	47	Vanderbilt	36,000
12	Tennessee, Memphis Med	41,000	47	Rochester	36,000
13	Yale	40,400	47	Minnesota	36,000
14	Wayne State	40,000	47	Louisville	36,000
14	Texas A&M	40,000	51	British Columbia	35,768
14	SUNY Stony Brook	40,000	52	Manitoba	35,083
14	Pennsylvania	40,000	53	Howard	35,049
14	Ohio State	40,000	54	Southern Illinois	35,000
14	Michigan	40,000	54	Nebraska	35,000
14	Iowa	40,000	54	Cincinnati	35,000
14	Florida	40,000	54	Case Western Reserve	35,000
22	Pittsburgh	39,000	54	Alabama	35,000
22	Pennsylvania State	39,000	59	Queen's	34,738
24	Washington	38,800	60	South Carolina	34,000
25	Montreal	38,771	60	Oklahoma State	34,000
26	SUNY Buffalo	38,753	60	Florida State	34,000
27	Boston University	38,500	63	Saskatchewan	33,453
28	Texas Tech	38,388	64	Utah	33,000
29	Washington-St. Louis	38,000	65	McGill	32,808
29	Tennessee, Knoxville Med	38,000	66	Kansas	32,800
29	Northwestern	38,000	67	McMaster	32,646
29	Miami	38,000	68	Missouri	32,500
29	Georgetown	38,000	69	Tulane	31,500
34	Calif. San Diego	37,920	70	Louisiana State	31,000
34	Calif. Los Angeles	37,920	71	Oklahoma	30,000
34	Calif. Irvine	37,920			

* Beginning salary figures represent officially designated base, not necessarily salaries of actual incumbents.
† Canadian salaries expressed in U.S. dollars.

TABLE 37: MEDIAN PROFESSIONAL SALARIES
IN ARL UNIVERSITY MEDICAL LIBRARIES
RANK ORDER TABLE, FY 2005-06*

Rank	Institution	Salary	Rank	Institution	Salary
1	Toronto	$72,063	34	Columbia	$52,034
2	Cornell	69,443	35	Pennsylvania	51,877
3	Southern California	69,071	36	Emory	51,838
4	Alberta	68,610	37	Wisconsin	51,805
5	Connecticut	68,386	38	Kentucky	51,683
6	California, Davis	66,558	39	Dartmouth	51,349
7	New Mexico	65,279	40	McGill	51,205
8	California, Los Angeles	64,332	41	Michigan	51,036
9	Case Western Reserve	62,647	42	Vanderbilt	50,851
10	New York University	62,412	43	Montreal	50,583
11	Yale	62,178	44	Oklahoma	50,551
12	Harvard	62,009	45	Nebraska	50,470
13	California, San Diego	60,100	46	Pennsylvania State	50,364
14	Northwestern	58,856	47	Temple	49,849
15	SUNY Stony Brook	58,490	48	Queen`s	49,317
16	Virginia	58,400	49	Louisville	49,289
17	Miami	57,960	50	Utah	49,157
18	Ohio State	56,968	51	Pittsburgh	48,885
19	Minnesota	56,950	52	McMaster	48,783
20	Cincinnati	56,757	53	Tennessee, Memphis	48,543
21	North Carolina	56,734	54	Iowa	48,465
22	Georgetown	55,944	55	Howard	47,769
23	Boston University	55,593	56	Rochester	47,247
24	George Washington	55,342	57	Washington U.-St. Louis	46,996
25	Johns Hopkins	55,221	58	Manitoba	46,576
26	British Columbia	55,069	59	Kansas	44,716
27	Southern Illinois	54,624	60	Texas Tech	43,527
28	Florida	54,497	61	Tennessee, Knoxville	41,889
29	Duke	54,349	62	Missouri	41,484
30	SUNY Buffalo	53,760	63	Tulane	41,200
31	Washington	53,640	64	Wayne State	40,918
32	Arizona	53,398	65	Saskatchewan	40,665
33	Illinois, Chicago	52,994	66	South Carolina	37,262

* Salaries of directors are not included in the calculation of medians. Alabama, California-Irvine, Florida State, Louisiana State, and Oklahoma
    State are not ranked because they reported fewer than four individuals.
† Canadian salaries expressed in U.S. dollars.

TABLE 38: AVERAGE PROFESSIONAL SALARIES
IN ARL UNIVERSITY MEDICAL LIBRARIES
RANK ORDER TABLE, FY 2005-06*

Rank	Institution	Salary	Rank	Institution	Salary
1	New Mexico	$73,591	34	Michigan	$54,690
2	Connecticut	70,790	35	Boston University	54,414
3	Cornell	69,764	36	Georgetown	54,262
4	California, San Diego	69,644	37	Duke	54,227
5	Southern California	68,518	38	Pennsylvania State	54,072
6	California, Davis	68,072	39	Florida	53,641
7	California, Los Angeles	66,956	40	British Columbia	53,595
8	Alberta	66,311	41	Wisconsin	53,295
9	Toronto	66,310	42	Pittsburgh	52,648
10	New York University	65,936	43	Southern Illinois	52,609
11	Harvard	65,437	44	McMaster	52,546
12	Yale	65,228	45	Tennessee, Memphis	52,526
13	Johns Hopkins	62,208	46	Vanderbilt	52,454
14	Cincinnati	61,046	47	Utah	52,380
15	Minnesota	59,938	48	Dartmouth	52,046
16	SUNY Stony Brook	59,816	49	Kentucky	51,939
17	Miami	59,807	50	McGill	51,616
18	George Washington	59,222	51	Louisville	51,613
19	Arizona	58,226	52	Rochester	51,213
20	Case Western Reserve	58,167	53	Montreal	51,007
21	Ohio State	58,112	54	Queen`s	50,766
22	Illinois, Chicago	57,895	55	Manitoba	50,152
23	Washington	57,618	56	Howard	50,145
24	Washington U.-St. Louis	57,283	57	Oklahoma	48,889
25	Iowa	56,853	58	Temple	48,726
26	North Carolina	56,808	59	Texas Tech	47,004
27	Nebraska	56,569	60	Kansas	46,601
28	Virginia	56,036	61	Tulane	45,508
29	Northwestern	55,919	62	Wayne State	43,963
30	Pennsylvania	55,505	63	Saskatchewan	43,731
31	Columbia	55,400	64	Missouri	42,498
32	Emory	55,385	65	South Carolina	41,788
33	SUNY Buffalo	55,304	66	Tennessee, Knoxville	41,525

* Salaries of directors are not included in the calculation of averages. Alabama, California-Irvine, Florida State, Louisiana State, and Oklahoma State are not ranked because they reported fewer than four individuals.

† Canadian salaries expressed in U.S. dollars.

TABLE 39: NUMBER AND AVERAGE SALARIES OF ARL UNIVERSITY MEDICAL LIBRARIANS BY POSITION AND SEX, FY 2005-06

Position	Women Salary	Women No.	Men Salary	Men No.	Total Salary	Total No.
Head, Medical	$108,532	38	$126,308	19	$114,458	57
Associate Director	79,118	43	85,460	16	80,838	59
Assistant Director	63,843	37	57,149	6	62,909	43
Head, Branch	59,324	32	71,395	4	60,666	36
Functional Specialist	51,759	79	55,205	64	53,302	143
Subject Specialist	55,317	32	54,565	4	55,234	36
Dept. Head: Acquisitions	†	13	†	3	59,999	16
Reference	64,723	18	64,425	12	64,604	30
Cataloging	†	9	†	1	60,600	10
Serials	†	7	†	1	55,820	8
Documents/Maps	†	1	†	1	†	2
Circulation	58,645	9	66,400	5	61,415	14
Rare Books/Manuscripts	71,681	8	71,377	5	71,564	13
Computer Systems	65,712	7	76,019	8	71,209	15
Other	61,739	53	64,115	14	62,236	67
Reference: Over 14 years experience	54,238	93	60,391	16	55,141	109
10 to 14 years experience	49,606	38	52,473	10	50,203	48
5 to 9 years experience	48,607	37	56,745	12	50,600	49
Under 5 years experience	42,558	57	46,940	12	43,320	69
Cataloging: Over 14 years experience	†	8	†	1	48,275	9
10 to 14 years experience	†	2	†	2	53,201	4
5 to 9 years experience	†	3	†	1	43,494	4
Under 5 years experience	†	3	N/A		†	3
Other: Over 14 years experience	60,251	21	53,150	7	58,476	28
10 to 14 years experience	47,986	5	51,293	5	49,640	10
5 to 9 years experience	48,611	13	43,020	4	47,296	17
Under 5 years experience	†	11	†	3	41,948	14
All Positions	**$58,895**	**677**	**$65,008**	**236**	**$60,475**	**913**

* Canadian salaries expressed in U.S. dollars.
† Salary data are not published when fewer than four individuals are involved in either category.
N/A - No positions were reported in this category.

TABLE 40: NUMBER AND AVERAGE YEARS OF EXPERIENCE OF ARL UNIVERSITY MEDICAL LIBRARIANS BY POSITION AND SEX, FY 2005-06

Position	Women		Men		Total	
	Years	No.	Years	No.	Years	No.
Head, Medical	28.7	38	27.2	19	28.2	57
Associate Director	23.8	43	23.6	16	23.7	59
Assistant Director	19.5	37	13.2	6	18.6	43
Head, Branch	18.3	32	26.0	4	19.1	36
Functional Specialist	13.5	79	10.6	64	12.2	143
Subject Specialist	15.3	32	9.8	4	14.7	36
Dept. Head: Acquisitions	19.8	13	29.3	3	21.6	16
Reference	22.9	18	19.6	12	21.6	30
Cataloging	17.6	9	29.0	1	18.7	10
Serials	27.1	7	28.0	1	27.3	8
Documents/Maps	15.0	1	11.0	1	13.0	2
Circulation	18.2	9	6.2	5	13.9	14
Rare Books/Manuscripts	24.9	8	23.2	5	24.2	13
Computer Systems	12.9	7	16.6	8	14.9	15
Other	20.1	53	14.1	14	18.8	67
Public Services	14.6	27	12.3	10	14.0	37
Technical Services	14.5	11	15.8	4	14.9	15
Administrative Services	19.2	12	18.8	5	19.1	17
Reference	13.3	225	11.9	50	13.1	275
Cataloger	14.8	16	15.3	4	14.9	20
All Positions	**17.1**	**677**	**15.3**	**236**	**16.6**	**913**

N/A - No positions were reported in this category.

TABLE 41: NUMBER AND AVERAGE SALARIES OF
ARL UNIVERSITY MEDICAL LIBRARIANS
BY YEARS OF EXPERIENCE AND SEX, FY 2005-06*

| Experience | Women | | Men | | Total | | % of |
	Salary	No.	Salary	No.	Salary	No.	Total
0 - 3 years	$44,345	81	$47,095	25	$44,994	106	12%
4 - 7 years	48,289	98	54,598	46	50,304	144	16%
8 - 11 years	54,542	73	60,025	35	56,319	108	12%
12 - 15 years	53,926	67	60,054	23	55,492	90	10%
16 - 19 years	55,896	62	71,918	23	60,231	85	9%
20 - 23 years	61,133	83	71,566	23	63,397	106	12%
24 - 27 years	66,273	74	73,870	24	68,134	98	11%
28 - 31 years	72,656	68	82,668	21	75,018	89	10%
32 - 35 years	82,290	44	81,537	11	82,139	55	6%
over 35 years	72,157	27	92,972	5	75,409	32	4%
All Positions	**$58,895**	**677**	**$65,008**	**236**	**$60,475**	**913**	**100%**

* Canadian salaries expressed in U.S. dollars.
† Salary data are not published when fewer than four individuals are involved in either category.

ARL UNIVERSITY LAW LIBRARIES

Tables 42–48

TABLE 42: FILLED POSITIONS; AVERAGE, MEDIAN, BEGINNING PROFESSIONAL SALARIES; AND AVERAGE YEARS OF EXPERIENCE
IN ARL UNIVERSITY LAW LIBRARIES, FY 2005-06*

Institution	Filled Positions	Average Salary	Median Salary	Beginning Salary	Average Yrs. Exp.
Alabama	10	61,683	56,650	35,000	17.0
Alberta	3	‡	‡	36,366	25.7
Arizona	11	57,218	58,082	47,000	16.1
Arizona State	7	57,571	57,146	38,000	18.7
Boston University	10	65,000	55,500	50,000	18.2
Boston College	14	67,681	73,050	38,700	20.6
British Columbia	3	‡	‡	35,768	18.0
California, Davis	7	73,967	73,290	37,920	22.9
California, Los Angeles	14	71,588	70,500	37,920	15.6
Case Western Reserve	12	60,704	60,256	35,000	15.9
Cincinnati	9	55,746	56,779	38,106	19.6
Colorado	8	62,470	52,730	38,000	15.4
Columbia	16	68,715	68,105	52,500	14.3
Connecticut	11	64,716	65,877	36,830	15.3
Cornell	8	63,278	59,590	50,000	13.3
Duke	10	66,194	67,100	45,000	16.7
Emory	10	54,839	52,180	37,000	15.1
Florida	9	55,267	51,678	40,000	22.8
Florida State	9	48,527	49,116	35,000	20.7
George Washington	20	65,780	65,143	50,000	12.9
Georgetown	22	72,353	67,100	42,000	13.4
Georgia	8	47,436	45,561	36,000	13.8
Harvard	43	71,870	71,192	43,600	19.7
Hawaii	5	60,075	57,709	40,000	12.4
Houston	13	52,660	49,761	48,000	12.9
Howard	9	42,831	43,921	35,049	16.3
Illinois, Urbana	9	58,339	58,642	51,000	13.2
Indiana	10	61,048	57,171	36,227	17.5
Iowa	17	65,535	59,750	40,000	19.4
Kansas	7	46,356	39,423	29,411	7.7
Kentucky	6	46,133	41,376	37,500	8.0
Louisiana State	8	55,788	48,599	40,000	20.6
Louisville	5	61,899	55,094	36,000	18.0
McGill	5	57,091	62,894	32,808	23.8
Manitoba	3	‡	‡	35,083	26.3
Miami	16	52,750	52,000	38,000	15.3
Michigan	10	75,721	74,091	46,250	19.9
Minnesota	14	66,456	60,389	40,000	17.9
Missouri	7	44,472	45,289	35,000	10.0

* Directors are included in figures for average years of experience and filled positions, but not in either the average or median salary statistic.
† Canadian salaries expressed in U.S. dollars.
‡ Salary data are not published when fewer than four individuals are involved.   U/A - Unavailable
§ See Footnotes.

TABLE 42: FILLED POSITIONS; AVERAGE, MEDIAN, BEGINNING PROFESSIONAL SALARIES; AND AVERAGE YEARS OF EXPERIENCE
IN ARL UNIVERSITY LAW LIBRARIES, FY 2005-06*

Institution	Filled Positions	Average Salary	Median Salary	Beginning Salary	Average Yrs. Exp.
Montreal	6	50,341	50,583	38,771	16.5
Nebraska	5	53,875	53,500	30,000	13.4
New Mexico	6	65,962	60,171	47,000	14.7
New York University	19	70,654	68,035	54,000	18.1
North Carolina	12	62,106	57,324	40,000	15.1
Northwestern	12	61,465	57,000	39,000	17.6
Notre Dame	12	62,922	56,300	36,000	18.2
Ohio State	7	62,124	58,000	40,000	16.9
Oklahoma	7	49,400	44,359	36,000	12.7
Oregon	5	52,091	48,192	37,000	18.8
Pennsylvania	14	63,054	58,550	40,000	15.4
Pennsylvania State	6	61,778	62,304	39,000	19.8
Queen`s	3	‡	‡	34,738	18.0
Rutgers, Camden	9	60,292	65,500	52,000	18.7
Rutgers, Newark	9	57,874	52,117	45,358	15.3
Saskatchewan	3	‡	‡	33,453	18.0
South Carolina	7	58,744	58,573	49,000	13.9
Southern Illinois	6	63,702	57,024	45,000	20.0
SUNY Buffalo	13	58,618	65,691	38,753	17.8
Syracuse	9	54,069	49,747	40,000	17.0
Temple	10	55,432	47,520	36,500	20.5
Tennessee	9	63,206	60,240	36,000	21.6
Texas	15	58,403	51,700	37,000	19.2
Texas Tech	7	50,263	49,241	35,000	11.9
Toronto	6	67,092	67,143	36,649	13.7
Tulane	9	56,712	52,556	35,000	17.4
Utah	8	55,347	57,786	40,000	20.0
Vanderbilt	7	56,854	54,473	36,000	18.3
Virginia	12	59,973	59,500	47,000	15.7
Washington	17	62,383	62,118	48,000	19.3
Washington U.-St. Louis	9	58,089	56,813	46,000	15.4
Wayne State	9	42,475	42,875	40,000	11.4
Western Ontario	4	46,150	44,254	37,185	15.8
Wisconsin	13	57,363	54,492	37,719	20.2
Yale	18	71,102	65,788	40,400	20.7
York	5	69,540	69,406	33,788	26.0

* Directors are included in figures for average years of experience and filled positions, but not in either the average or median salary statistic.
† Canadian salaries expressed in U.S. dollars.
‡ Salary data are not published when fewer than four individuals are involved.   U/A - Unavailable
§ See Footnotes.

TABLE 43: BEGINNING PROFESSIONAL SALARIES
IN ARL UNIVERSITY LAW LIBRARIES
RANK ORDER TABLE, FY 2005-06*

Rank	Institution	Salary	Rank	Institution	Salary
1	New York	$54,000	39	Arizona State	$38,000
2	Columbia	52,500	39	Colorado	38,000
3	Rutgers, Camden Law	52,000	39	Miami	38,000
4	Illinois, Urbana	51,000	42	Calif. Davis	37,920
5	Boston University	50,000	42	Calif. Los Angeles	37,920
5	Cornell	50,000	44	Wisconsin	37,719
5	George Washington	50,000	45	Kentucky	37,500
8	South Carolina	49,000	46	Western Ontario	37,185
9	Houston	48,000	47	Emory	37,000
9	Washington	48,000	47	Oregon	37,000
11	Arizona	47,000	47	Texas	37,000
11	New Mexico	47,000	50	Connecticut	36,830
11	Virginia	47,000	51	Toronto	36,649
14	Michigan	46,250	52	Temple	36,500
15	Washington-St. Louis	46,000	53	Alberta	36,366
16	Rutgers, Newark Law	45,358	54	Indiana	36,227
17	Duke	45,000	55	Georgia	36,000
17	Southern Illinois	45,000	55	Louisville	36,000
19	Harvard	43,600	55	Notre Dame	36,000
20	Georgetown	42,000	55	Oklahoma	36,000
21	Yale	40,400	55	Tennessee	36,000
22	Florida	40,000	55	Vanderbilt	36,000
22	Hawaii	40,000	61	British Columbia	35,768
22	Iowa	40,000	62	Manitoba	35,083
22	Louisiana State	40,000	63	Howard	35,049
22	Minnesota	40,000	64	Alabama	35,000
22	North Carolina	40,000	64	Case Western Reserve	35,000
22	Ohio State	40,000	64	Florida State	35,000
22	Pennsylvania	40,000	64	Missouri	35,000
22	Syracuse	40,000	64	Texas Tech	35,000
22	Utah	40,000	64	Tulane	35,000
22	Wayne State	40,000	70	Queen's	34,738
33	Northwestern	39,000	71	York	33,788
33	Pennsylvania State	39,000	72	Saskatchewan	33,453
35	Montreal	38,771	73	McGill	32,808
36	SUNY Buffalo	38,753	74	Nebraska	30,000
37	Boston College	38,700	75	Kansas	29,411
38	Cincinnati	38,106			

* Beginning salary figures represent officially designated base, not necessarily salaries of actual incumbents.
† Canadian salaries expressed in U.S. dollars.

TABLE 44: MEDIAN PROFESSIONAL SALARIES
IN ARL UNIVERSITY LAW LIBRARIES
RANK ORDER TABLE, FY 2005-06*

Rank	Institution	Salary	Rank	Institution	Salary
1	Michigan	$74,091	36	Arizona State	$57,146
2	California, Davis	73,290	37	Southern Illinois	57,024
3	Boston College	73,050	38	Northwestern	57,000
4	Harvard	71,192	39	Washington U.-St. Louis	56,813
5	California, Los Angeles	70,500	40	Cincinnati	56,779
6	York	69,406	41	Alabama	56,650
7	Columbia	68,105	42	Notre Dame	56,300
8	New York University	68,035	43	Boston University	55,500
9	Toronto	67,143	44	Louisville	55,094
10	Duke	67,100	45	Wisconsin	54,492
10	Georgetown	67,100	46	Vanderbilt	54,473
12	Connecticut	65,877	47	Nebraska	53,500
13	Yale	65,788	48	Colorado	52,730
14	SUNY Buffalo	65,691	49	Tulane	52,556
15	Rutgers, Camden	65,500	50	Emory	52,180
16	George Washington	65,143	51	Rutgers, Newark	52,117
17	McGill	62,894	52	Miami	52,000
18	Pennsylvania State	62,304	53	Texas	51,700
19	Washington	62,118	54	Florida	51,678
20	Minnesota	60,389	55	Montreal	50,583
21	Case Western Reserve	60,256	56	Houston	49,761
22	Tennessee	60,240	57	Syracuse	49,747
23	New Mexico	60,171	58	Texas Tech	49,241
24	Iowa	59,750	59	Florida State	49,116
25	Cornell	59,590	60	Louisiana State	48,599
26	Virginia	59,500	61	Oregon	48,192
27	Illinois, Urbana	58,642	62	Temple	47,520
28	South Carolina	58,573	63	Georgia	45,561
29	Pennsylvania	58,550	64	Missouri	45,289
30	Arizona	58,082	65	Oklahoma	44,359
31	Ohio State	58,000	66	Western Ontario	44,254
32	Utah	57,786	67	Howard	43,921
33	Hawaii	57,709	68	Wayne State	42,875
34	North Carolina	57,324	69	Kentucky	41,376
35	Indiana	57,171	70	Kansas	39,423

* Salaries of directors are not included in the calculation of medians. Alberta, Manitoba, Queen's, and Saskatchewan are not ranked because they reported fewer than four individuals.

† Canadian salaries expressed in U.S. dollars.

TABLE 45: AVERAGE PROFESSIONAL SALARIES IN ARL UNIVERSITY LAW LIBRARIES RANK ORDER TABLE, FY 2005-06*

Rank	Institution	Salary	Rank	Institution	Salary
1	Michigan	$75,721	36	Virginia	$59,973
2	California, Davis	73,967	37	South Carolina	58,744
3	Georgetown	72,353	38	SUNY Buffalo	58,618
4	Harvard	71,870	39	Texas	58,403
5	California, Los Angeles	71,588	40	Illinois, Urbana	58,339
6	Yale	71,102	41	Washington U.-St. Louis	58,089
7	New York University	70,654	42	Rutgers, Newark	57,874
8	York	69,540	43	Arizona State	57,571
9	Columbia	68,715	44	Wisconsin	57,363
10	Boston College	67,681	45	Arizona	57,218
11	Toronto	67,092	46	McGill	57,091
12	Minnesota	66,456	47	Vanderbilt	56,854
13	Duke	66,194	48	Tulane	56,712
14	New Mexico	65,962	49	Louisiana State	55,788
15	George Washington	65,780	50	Cincinnati	55,746
16	Iowa	65,535	51	Temple	55,432
17	Boston University	65,000	52	Utah	55,347
18	Connecticut	64,716	53	Florida	55,267
19	Southern Illinois	63,702	54	Emory	54,839
20	Cornell	63,278	55	Syracuse	54,069
21	Tennessee	63,206	56	Nebraska	53,875
22	Pennsylvania	63,054	57	Miami	52,750
23	Notre Dame	62,922	58	Houston	52,660
24	Colorado	62,470	59	Oregon	52,091
25	Washington	62,383	60	Montreal	50,341
26	Ohio State	62,124	61	Texas Tech	50,263
27	North Carolina	62,106	62	Oklahoma	49,400
28	Louisville	61,899	63	Florida State	48,527
29	Pennsylvania State	61,778	64	Georgia	47,436
30	Alabama	61,683	65	Kansas	46,356
31	Northwestern	61,465	66	Western Ontario	46,150
32	Indiana	61,048	67	Kentucky	46,133
33	Case Western Reserve	60,704	68	Missouri	44,472
34	Rutgers, Camden	60,292	69	Howard	42,831
35	Hawaii	60,075	70	Wayne State	42,475

* Salaries of directors are not included in the calculation of averages. Alberta, Manitoba, Queen's, and Saskatchewan are not ranked because they reported fewer than four individuals.
† Canadian salaries expressed in U.S. dollars.

TABLE 46: NUMBER AND AVERAGE SALARIES OF
ARL UNIVERSITY LAW LIBRARIANS
BY POSITION AND SEX, FY 2005-06*

Position	Women		Men		Total	
	Salary	No.	Salary	No.	Salary	No.
Head, Law	$131,576	35	$145,257	38	$138,698	73
Associate Director	88,856	34	85,541	21	87,591	55
Assistant Director	76,717	22	79,828	9	77,620	31
Head, Branch	N/A		†	1	†	1
Functional Specialist	52,525	32	52,581	28	52,551	60
Subject Specialist	67,780	21	62,046	13	65,588	34
Dept. Head: Acquisitions	57,856	21	56,640	9	57,491	30
Reference	73,700	16	70,897	11	72,558	27
Cataloging	†	33	†	2	62,013	35
Serials	†	10	†	3	60,540	13
Documents/Maps	†	11	†	1	54,853	12
Circulation	58,865	24	52,273	10	56,926	34
Rare Books/Manuscripts	†	3	†	3	64,109	6
Computer Systems	53,923	6	66,398	6	60,161	12
Other	67,017	18	69,081	13	67,882	31
Reference: Over 14 years experience	61,557	48	61,767	22	61,623	70
10 to 14 years experience	58,736	22	60,771	7	59,227	29
5 to 9 years experience	53,746	25	54,798	19	54,200	44
Under 5 years experience	50,736	43	48,035	25	49,743	68
Cataloging: Over 14 years experience	59,121	22	61,736	8	59,818	30
10 to 14 years experience	†	9	†	1	46,129	10
5 to 9 years experience	†	1	†	1	†	2
Under 5 years experience	†	7	†	1	46,265	8
Other: Over 14 years experience	55,817	13	54,265	4	55,451	17
10 to 14 years experience	†	1	†	1	†	2
5 to 9 years experience	45,873	5	N/A		45,873	5
Under 5 years experience	†	5	†	2	44,057	7
All Positions	**$66,263**	**487**	**$73,960**	**259**	**$68,935**	**746**

* Canadian salaries expressed in U.S. dollars.
N/A - No positions were reported in this category.
† Salary data are not published when fewer than four individuals are involved in either category.

TABLE 47: NUMBER AND AVERAGE YEARS OF EXPERIENCE OF ARL UNIVERSITY LAW LIBRARIANS BY POSITION AND SEX, FY 2005-06

Position	Women		Men		Total	
	Years	No.	Years	No.	Years	No.
Head, Law	27.6	35	25.3	38	26.4	73
Associate Director	23.1	34	17.8	21	21.1	55
Assistant Director	21.6	22	20.0	9	21.2	31
Head, Branch	N/A		20.0	1	20.0	1
Functional Specialist	12.6	32	9.2	28	11.0	60
Subject Specialist	19.5	21	18.5	13	19.1	34
Dept. Head: Acquisitions	20.6	21	13.3	9	18.4	30
Reference	18.2	16	18.0	11	18.1	27
Cataloging	21.9	33	11.5	2	21.3	35
Serials	21.1	10	10.0	3	18.5	13
Documents/Maps	22.9	11	8.0	1	21.7	12
Circulation	16.3	24	10.2	10	14.5	34
Rare Books/Manuscripts	19.0	3	14.7	3	16.8	6
Computer Systems	14.3	6	19.3	6	16.8	12
Other	20.1	18	16.5	13	18.6	31
Public Services	18.8	8	12.0	2	17.4	10
Technical Services	17.6	9	24.5	2	18.8	11
Administrative Services	12.1	7	11.7	3	12.0	10
Reference	13.0	138	10.4	73	12.1	211
Cataloger	18.5	39	20.4	11	18.9	50
All Positions	**18.0**	**487**	**15.4**	**259**	**17.1**	**746**

TABLE 48: NUMBER AND AVERAGE SALARIES OF
ARL UNIVERSITY LAW LIBRARIANS
BY YEARS OF EXPERIENCE AND SEX, FY 2005-06*

| Experience | Women | | Men | | Total | | % of |
	Salary	No.	Salary	No.	Salary	No.	Total
0 - 3 years	$48,047	56	$46,957	34	$47,635	90	12%
4 - 7 years	52,949	48	53,528	45	53,229	93	12%
8 - 11 years	57,050	64	68,921	32	61,007	96	13%
12 - 15 years	60,027	52	65,390	25	61,768	77	10%
16 - 19 years	68,197	43	73,558	33	70,525	76	10%
20 - 23 years	70,772	45	92,991	22	78,068	67	9%
24 - 27 years	69,968	63	94,563	31	78,079	94	13%
28 - 31 years	81,547	60	91,052	21	84,011	81	11%
32 - 35 years	88,621	33	119,746	9	95,290	42	6%
over 35 years	83,607	23	130,788	7	94,616	30	4%
All Positions	**$66,263**	**487**	**$73,960**	**259**	**$68,935**	**746**	**100%**

* Canadian salaries expressed in U.S. dollars.

UNIVERSITY LIBRARY

Questionnaire and Instructions

ARL ANNUAL SALARY SURVEY 2005-06
UNIVERSITY LIBRARY QUESTIONNAIRE
General Instructions for Completing the Questionnaire

1. This survey is concerned with professional positions only. Since the criteria for determining professional status vary among libraries, there is no attempt to define the term "professional." Each library should report the salaries of those staff members it considers professionals, irrespective of faculty status or membership in a collective bargaining unit, including, when appropriate, staff who are not librarians in the strict sense of the term, such as computer experts, systems analysts, budget officers, etc.

2. Individual salaries for the general, law, and medical library may be reported on the templates (located online at ftp://www.arl.org/stat/salary/), using Microsoft Excel. See "Instructions for Data Input." Please **DO NOT alter** the formatted worksheets on the templates in any way; do not change any page or line numbers. If you are not able to produce data that can be saved on the templates, please submit your data using the printed forms. [If you have an Excel or word-processing file with your data in properly labeled columns, you may submit a printout of that file in lieu of the preprinted forms.]

3. Salaries should be reported for both full-time and part-time professional positions. Salaries for part-time positions should **NOT** be converted to their full-time equivalents; report the actual part-time salary paid, and indicate the percent appointment for that employee in the appropriate column.

4. To calculate the percent appointment, if less than 1.00, which stands for 100%, divide the months the employee works by the number of months considered to be the norm for full-time employment at your institution (or the number of hours per week an employee works by the number of hours per week considered to be the norm for full-time employment at your institution). For example, if a full-time appointment at your institution is 12 months, a 9-month part-time appointment would be .75, i.e. 75%. If a full-time appointment at your institution is 40 hours per week, an appointment at 30 hours per week is also .75. To calculate the percent appointment for an employee who works 30 hours a week and only for 9 months a year, when the norm for full-time employment is 40 hours a week and a 12-month appointment, multiply the percent appointment per week by the percent appointment per year, i.e. .75 x .75 = .56.

5. Percent appointment should be rounded to two decimal places; do NOT use whole numbers (e.g., enter .65, not 65 or 65%). All other numbers (e.g. salaries, years of experience) should be rounded to the **nearest whole number**.

6. The salaries for all professional positions should be included, regardless of whether the salaries come from regular library budget funds **or from special funds such as research grants**. Please include all professionals involved in the provision of library services, including **contract-supported positions**.

7. The salary figures should be straight gross salary figures. **Do not include fringe benefits**.

8. Salary figures should be reported in digits only; do NOT use "$" or "," (e.g., 25470, not $25,470).

9. Explanatory footnotes to the reported figures may be provided, when necessary, at the end of Part I. Footnotes will be included in the published survey, where appropriate.

10. After all data have been entered, make a backup copy of the complete file (including individual names/ID numbers) for your institution's master file, if you wish to refer to this file in the future. Note: The data submitted to ARL should NOT include individual names or ID numbers, so ARL will NOT be able to supply a copy of your institution's complete file next year.

11. The questionnaire should be returned to the ARL Office by **September 30, 2005**. If you are providing the individual data as an electronic file, please send the files as an email attachment to stats-ra@arl.org, and mail or

fax Part I of the survey and a printout of the data file (Part II). Alternatively, you can save the files on a disk and mail the disk with the hard copy of Part I and Part II of the survey. **Be sure to keep a complete copy of your return, including the electronic version of the data for your files**.

Instructions for Completing Part I: Summary Data

1. Part I of this survey deals with general information for the current fiscal year, 2005-06.

2. Please include the Beginning Professional Salary for Law and Medical libraries if included in the survey; if not included, enter "N/A" in the appropriate blank.

3. **Question 1**. The Beginning Professional Salary is the salary that **would** be paid to a **newly hired professional without experience**, not necessarily the lowest professional salary paid. In reporting the beginning salary, please use a figure that is actually used or likely to be used for entry-level librarians hired by your library, even if it is your practice rarely to hire entry-level professionals without experience.

   Please report the **2005-06** Beginning Professional Salary to the best of your knowledge as it exists on July 1, 2005. Do not delay returning your survey with the expectation that more information will be available later.

4. The 2005-06 Average and Median Salary figures will be calculated by ARL from the individual data supplied.

5. Be sure to fill in the name of the reporting library and the name of the person who prepares the report.

Instructions for Completing Part II: Individual Data

1. Part II of this survey requests information on salary, sex, minority status, rank, and years of experience for all filled positions for fiscal year 2005-06. The survey requests information for individuals; aggregate data for each institution will be generated by computer. Vacant positions should be excluded from your report.

2. Data for the general, law, and medical libraries may be reported on separate templates; see #4 below for specific instructions.

3. **Survey Form.** If you are not able to submit the data in electronic form, please use the enclosed forms. Photocopy additional sheets if you cannot list all professional positions in the space provided. You may also use a printout from a word-processing document with all columns correctly ordered and labeled.

   If you are reporting on paper forms only, list information for individuals in separate Law or Medical libraries on sheets devoted only to each of those two branches. Check the appropriate box at the top of the form to indicate when a sheet is only for Law or Medical library staff.

   The left-hand column labeled "Name/ID" has been provided so the form can also serve as a work sheet. **After the forms have been completed, the left-hand column should be removed to ensure anonymity of the data.** Except for segregating Law and Medical library staff, the order in which staff members are entered on the form is immaterial; enter them in the order most convenient for you.

4. **Template.** The templates contain data input files for general, law, and medical library data in .xls files that can be uploaded into spreadsheet programs. They are labeled as follows:

General	ARL05xxxx.xls
Law	LAW05xxxx.xls
Medical	MED05xxxx.xls

   xxxx = Library identification number; see label on the file. The file names this year have a "05" (standing for 2005-06) preceding the four-digit library identification number to distinguish them from, and prevent overwriting of, files you may have created in prior years.

The files contain empty worksheets with the required columns labeled as follows:

Name/ID LibID Page Line Salary Job Sex OEOcat Yrsexp Rank Percent

Every five years, data are tracked in the following five optional categories:

YrBirth JobAdd LibDeg OthDeg YrsLib

The final six columns, which are optional, are included in accordance with standards for the classification of federal data on race and ethnicity:

Hispanic or Latino
Amer. Indian or Alaska Native
Asian
Black or African-American
Native Hawaiian/Other Pacific Islander
White

The first entry in the column labeled "LibID" is already filled in so there will be no question about the institutional identity of the files as they are received. If the files have been damaged in any way or if the number in the LibID column is not the same as the library number at http://www.arl.org/stats/arlstat/instno_inam.html , please call the ARL Office for instructions.

Detailed instructions follow for inputting data in each format. **Please do not alter any formats, page or line numbers.** After all data have been entered, make a backup copy of the complete file (including individual names/ID numbers) for your institution's master file, if you wish to refer to this file in the future. Note: The data submitted to ARL does NOT include individual names or ID numbers, so ARL will NOT be able to supply a copy of your institution's complete file next year.

5.   **Salary.** Enter the individual salaries *as they exist* on July 1, 2005. If the library normally increases salaries at a date later than July 1, and the salary as of that later date is known or can be estimated (within $100 or so) by the time the questionnaire is due to be returned, use the higher salary figure and footnote the effective date and/or whether the reported figures are known or estimated. Please do not hold up the reporting process for later salary adjustments. Salaries should be reported for all filled positions. Vacant positions should be excluded from your report.

Salary figures should be rounded off to the nearest whole dollar. Use digits only; do NOT use "$" or "," in reporting in figures (e.g., 25470, not $25,470).

6.   **Position Code (Job).** The position categories used in this survey are intended to correspond roughly with the activities carried on in libraries, not with any particular pattern of staff organization or nomenclature. Please use these categories in the manner you feel best applies to your library. Indicate a position title by means of one of the following codes.

DIRLIB   Director of Libraries (or equivalent title; refers to chief executive)
ASCDIR   Associate Director
ASTDIR   Assistant Director
HDMED   Head, Medical Library (Human Medicine only)
HDLAW   Head, Law Library
HDBR   Head, Other Branch Library (including Veterinary Medicine)
FSPEC   Functional Specialist

ARCH	Archivists/Curators
BUSI	Budget/Fiscal/Business Manager/Facilities
HUMRES	Human Resources/Training/Staff Development
ITS	Information Technology Systems
ITW	Information Technology Web Development
ITP	Information Technology Programming/Applications Development
MEDIA	Media/Multimedia Specialists (including graphics)
PRES	Preservation/Conservation
SSPEC	Subject Specialist
HDACQ	Head, Acquisitions Department
HDCAT	Head, Catalog Department/Unit
HDCIRC	Head, Circulation
HDCOMP	Head, Library and Computer Systems
HDDOC	Head, Documents Department
HDMAP	Head, Map Room/Department
HDRBM	Head, Rare Book/Manuscripts Department
HDREF	Head, Reference Department
HDSER	Head, Serials Department
HDOTH	Head, Other Department/Service/Agency
CAT	Catalogers, both general and specialized
REF	Reference librarians, both general and specialized
PUBS	Public Services, non-supervisory, except reference librarians
TECH	Technical Services, non-supervisory, except catalogers
ADMIN	Administrative and other units, non-supervisory position

If any individual has responsibilities described by more than one of the above categories, choose the category that is most typical of his/her general duties. Codes must be used exactly as they appear in the list above.

Associate or Assistant Director, and Head, Other Branch. Use these codes for all persons at these levels regardless of the area of specialty. If an assistant or associate director is also head of a department, choose the category that most reflects the general duties of the person currently in the position.

Specialists. These are of two kinds: Subject Specialists primarily build collections, but may also offer specialized reference and bibliographic services; Functional Specialists are media specialists or experts in management fields such as personnel, fiscal matters, systems, preservation, etc. Specialists may not be, strictly speaking, professional librarians (i.e., have an MLS). The "specialist" category would generally not be used for someone with significant supervisory responsibilities, who should instead be listed as a department head or assistant director (see also note under Assistant Department Head, below).

Functional Specialist sub-categories. Starting with the 2004-05 *Salary Survey*, the ARL Statistics and Measurement Committee adopted a proposal from the ACRL Personnel Administrators and Staff Development Officers Discussion Group to break down the Functional Specialist category. For each position which would have been labeled FSPEC prior to 2004-05, instead please use one of the eight sub-codes (ARCH, BUSI, HUMRES, ITS, ITW, ITP, MEDIA, PRES) to describe that position. **Please use the sub-codes only for those positions which would have been labeled FSPEC prior to 2004-05. If it cannot be determined which sub-code to use, please use the FSPEC code.**

Department Heads. Department Heads not specifically included in the above list should be included under the category "Head, Other Department/Service/Agency." Head, Catalog Department should be used either for the department that handles all cataloging, or for the head of a specialized cataloging unit (e.g. copy cataloging or foreign languages). List the head of library automation and computer systems, applications, programming, etc. as HDCOMP unless that person is also an Associate or Assistant Director, in which case use the appropriate administrative code. If there is an intermediate level of management between an Associate or Assistant Director and the professionals who actually carry out the analysis, programming, etc., use HDCOMP to define that intermediate level. Professionals who carry out analysis, programming, etc. should be listed as functional specialists (FSPEC).

Head, Acquisitions Department. Use HDACQ for all of the following positions: (a) head of a department that is responsible for the selection of material (or management of selection activities carried out on a basis encompassing more than a single organizational unit), but not responsible for the placement of orders, payment of invoices, etc.; (b) head of a department responsible for the placement of orders, maintaining on-order files, payment of invoices, etc., but not responsible for selection decisions; (c) head of a department responsible for both the selection decisions (or coordination of selection activities) and for acquiring the material. Libraries that split these two functions between two departments should report more than one professional with the position HDACQ.

[*Special note concerning Assistant Department Heads.* Assistant Department Heads who are responsible for major units and spend the bulk of their time in supervision and revision of the work of others should also be listed as "Head, Other Department/Service/Agency." See additional subcodes below for Head, Cataloging, and Head, Other Department. However, Assistant Head positions responsible for small units or for supervision only in the absence of the head should be reported as non-supervisory or specialist positions as appropriate.]

Administrative. Please note that ADMIN is not only for Administrative Services and related positions, but also can be applied to Public Relations/Communications, Development/Fundraising, and all other administrative and/or professional positions which do not have a logical home elsewhere.

7.   **Sex.** Indicate either M or F, for male and female, respectively. Please use only the letter indicated; do not spell out the word.

8.   **Minority status code (OEOCat).** U.S. university libraries, only, should indicate minority status by means of one of the following code numbers. (Leave blank if a Canadian library or if vacant.)

   1 Black
   2 Hispanic
   3 Asian or Pacific Islander
   4 American Indian or Native Alaskan
   5 Caucasian/Other

9.   **Total years of professional experience (Yrsexp).** Define "professional experience" as indicated in the general instructions; for most professional staff members this will mean counting the years since the MLS degree was awarded. When counting, do not subtract interim periods when an individual was not engaged in professional library employment if these periods are short in relation to the overall professional career. Count an academic year contract period as a full year. Be sure to include professional experience in previous positions and in other institutions. Numbers should be rounded off to the nearest whole number.

10. **Rank.** Responses concerning rank should be limited to professional librarians, and other professionals who occupy the same ranks as librarians. Leave the rank column blank for professionals who do not occupy these ranks or if the column is not applicable. For example, if the Library Business Officer holds a rank typically used for university administrators but not for librarians, do not supply a rank code for that individual or describe his/her rank in answering other questions, even if you have included salary and other data for the Business Officer.

If multiple ranking structures are used for librarians and these structures are substantially different and not equivalent, enter individual rank information only for that group which represents the largest fraction of "rank-and-file" librarians.

<u>Do not use roman numeral rank levels. Convert your local ranking system if necessary.</u>

Complete the column labeled "Rank Code" using the following codes:

0	A rank normally occupied <u>solely</u> by the library director and/or assistant and associate directors.
9	Rank unknown; or, there is confusion or controversy regarding how to code this individual's rank.
1	Lowest level in the rank structure.
2	Next highest level in the rank structure.
3-8	Successively higher levels in the rank structure. Highest number in this range should be equivalent to the highest rank in the library's structure (unless the highest rank is occupied solely by the director and/or assistant and associate directors).

The maximum number of ranks reported here should not exceed the maximum number of rank-levels reported in Part I for individual data under Rank Structure.

When counting the total number of rank levels, include ranks that may be unoccupied at the present time due to circumstances like unusually high turnover, hiring freezes, etc.

11. **Percent.** Change the 100% appointment to less than that **only** for part-time people. Enter percent with decimal points. For example, a 65% appointment would be entered as .65. To calculate the percent appointment, if less than 1.00, which stands for 100%, divide the months the employee works by the number of months considered to be the norm for full-time employment at your institution (or the number of hours per week an employee works by the number of hours per week considered to be the norm for full-time employment at your institution). For example, if a full-time appointment at your institution is 12 months, a 9-month part-time appointment would be .75, i.e. 75%. If a full-time appointment at your institution is 40 hours per week, an appointment at 30 hours per week is also .75. To calculate the percent appointment for an employee who works 30 hours a week and only for 9 months a year, when the norm for full-time employment is 40 hours a week and a 12-month appointment, multiply the percent appointment per week by the percent appointment per year, i.e. .75 x .75 = .56.

Instructions for Completing Part III: Additional Categories
(Shown on printed forms as the last 11 columns)

1. **Year of Birth (YrBirth).** For each individual, record the four-digit year of birth.

2. **Position Code Addenda (JobAdd).** Use this column to provide additional information only for the following position categories.

    a. **Associate and Assistant Directors** (ASCDIR and ASTDIR). For each category, indicate if the person has a defined area of responsibility using the codes below. Use the code that most closely reflects the general duties of the person in the position.

Administrative Services	ADM	Systems/Automation	SYS
Collection Development	CDV	Technical Services	TS
Public Services	PBS	Other or unspec.	OTH

    b. **Head, Other Branch Library** (HDBR). Use the codes below to indicate the subject area of the branch:

Science & Tech.	SCI	Undergraduate Library	UGL
Social/Behavioral Sci.	SBS	Other	OTH
Humanities/Fine Arts	HFA		

c. **Functional Specialists** (FSPEC). Indicate any non-supervisory staff who are primarily responsible for the following activities using the codes below:

Acquisitions	ACQ	Development Officer	DVP
Interlibrary Loan	ILL	Marketing/Communications	COM
Serials	SER		

d. **Subject Specialists, Reference Librarians, Catalogers, and Public Services** (SSPEC, REF, CAT, PUBS). Use these codes to indicate non-supervisory main and/or branch library staff who specialize in <u>one</u> of the following subject areas (either a sub-field, or the entire area). Do not add codes for staff in these positions who have broader, other, or mixed subject responsibilities (e.g. more than one field specialty); but do include subject specialists who also have some (i.e. 50% or less) general or other assignments.

Science & Tech.	SCI	Humanities/Fine Arts	HFA
Social/Behavioral Sci.	SBS	Undergraduate Library	UGL

e. **Head, Cataloging Department/Unit** (HDCAT). Use the codes below to indicate whether the person is the head of the entire cataloging department for the library, or the head of a specialized unit. If the person is head of the whole department, repeat the same HDCAT code as in the earlier column.

Head, all cataloging	HDCAT	Head, foreign languages	HDF
Head, copy cataloging	HDC	Head, non-book formats	HDN
Head, serials cat.	HDS	Head, other special cat.	HDO

f. **Head, Other Department/Service/Agency** (HDOTH). For heads of departments not given a separate category in the major list, please add one of the following codes:

Audio Visual/Media	AVM	Business/Personnel Office	BPO
Preservation	PRS	Other	OTH
Interlibrary Loan LL	Archivist	ARC	

3. **Library degrees earned (LibDeg).** Use the following codes to indicate the highest academic degree earned in the field of librarianship:

0	None
1	Bachelor
2	Master
3	CAGS (6th yr. certificate)
4	Doctorate (Other than Ph.D.)
5	Ph.D.

4. **Other degrees earned (OtherDeg).** Use the following codes to indicate the highest degree earned in fields other than librarianship, including basic undergraduate education:

0	None
1	Bachelor
2	Master
3	Second Master (i.e., 2 subject fields)
4	CAGS (6th-year certificate)
5	LLB/JD
6	Doctorate (Other than Ph.D.)
7	Ph.D.

5. **Years of professional experience at reporting institution (YrsLib).** Use this line to report the number of years of <u>professional</u> experience each librarian has had at your institution. This figure should not exceed the number reported as Total Years of Professional Experience on the main part of the form.

6. Please complete as much of this section as possible (US libraries only), but do not hold up the reporting process if some of the data requested are not available. Canadian libraries should leave these columns blank. The major change in the revised standard for the classification of federal data on race and ethnicity is that now respondents are able to report more than one race by choosing multiple responses to the following questions.

7. **Ethnicity:** U.S. university libraries, only, should indicate Hispanic or Latino ethnicity by coding 1 to indicate the presence of the characteristic (1=yes) and 0 to indicate its absence. The definition of Hispanic or Latino ethnicity is: A person of Cuban, Mexican, Puerto Rican, Cuban, South or Central American, or other Spanish culture or origin, regardless of race.

8. **Race:** U.S. university libraries, only, should indicate race by choosing one or more responses among the five racial categories provided here. The definitions of the five racial categories are:

American Indian or Alaska Native (NatAm): A person having origins in any of the original peoples of North and South America (including Central America) who maintains tribal affiliation or community attachment.

Asian (Asian): A person having origins in any of the original peoples of the Far East, Southeast Asia, or the Indian subcontinent including, for example, Cambodia, China, India, Japan, Korea, Malaysia, Pakistan, the Philippine Islands, Thailand, and Vietnam.

Black or African American (Black): A person having origins in any of the black racial groups of Africa.

Native Hawaiian or Other Pacific Islander (HawPI). A person having origins in any of the original peoples of Hawaii, Guam, Samoa, or other Pacific Islands.

White (White): A person having origins in any of the original peoples of Europe, the Middle East, or North Africa.

The presence or absence of a racial characteristics should be indicated by coding 1=yes and 0=no. You can select multiple racial categories for a person:

1= yes 0 = no American Indian or Native Alaska (AI/NA)
1= yes 0 = no Asian
1= yes 0 = no Black or African American
1= yes 0 = no Native Hawaiian or Other Pacific Islander (NH/OPI)
1= yes 0 = no White

ARL Annual Salary Survey 2005-06
University Library Questionnaire

Part I: Summary Data

Reporting Institution _____ Date Returned to ARL _____

Report Prepared by (name) _____

Title _____

Email address _____ Phone number _____

Contact person (if different) _____

Title _____

Email address _____ Phone number _____

		Main	Law	Medical
1.	**Beginning Professional Salary**			
	Beginning professional salary for 2005-06	_____	_____	_____

*(**Note:** ARL will calculate the **2005-06 median and average** professional salaries for your library from the individual data you supply in Part II of this questionnaire.)*

2.   **Rank Structure**.

Indicate the number of levels in your institution's rank structure for professional librarians. You should report here the maximum number of rank levels, reported in Part II for individual data, under the Rank column.

_____ 1 level (i.e., no differentiated levels)

_____ 2 levels

_____ 3 levels

_____ 4 levels

_____ 5 levels

_____ more than 5 levels (please specify the number of levels: _____)

3.   FOOTNOTES

3a. Please list which libraries are included in the data submitted for the "general" libraries. These can be main campus libraries or branch campus libraries.

3b. Please list which libraries are NOT included in the data submitted for the "general" libraries. These can be main campus libraries or branch campus libraries.

Please indicate any other explanatory information in footnotes. These additional footnotes, if necessary, should be placed in the space below or on attached pages.

Please return the completed questionnaire to the
ARL Statistics and Measurement Program by **September 30, 2005.**
For assistance, contact Martha Kyrillidou (martha@arl.org) or Mark Young (stats-ra@arl.org), or call 202-296-2296.

ARL ANNUAL SALARY SURVEY 2005-06
UNIVERSITY LIBRARY QUESTIONNAIRE
Part II: Individual Data

Reporting Library _____

Confidential
Detach before mailing to the ARL Office
Name/ID

Line	Salary	Job	Sex	OEO cat	Yrs Exp	Rank	% App	Year Birth	Job Add	Lib Deg	Other Deg	Yrs. Lib.	Ethnicity Hispanic or Latino	Race: NatAm	Race: Asian	Race: Black	Race: HawPI	Race: White
1																		
2																		
3																		
4																		
5																		
6																		
7																		
8																		
9																		
10																		
11																		
12																		
13																		
14																		
15																		
16																		
17																		
18																		
19																		
20																		
21																		
22																		
23																		
24																		
25																		

Duplicate this sheet if you need additional lines. Please return to the ARL Statistics and Measurement Program by **September 30, 2005**. For assistance, contact Martha Kyrillidou (martha@arl.org) or Mark Young (stats-ra@arl.org), or call 202-296-2296.

NONUNIVERSITY LIBRARY

Questionnaire and Instructions

ARL ANNUAL SALARY SURVEY 2005-06
NONUNIVERSITY LIBRARY QUESTIONNAIRE
General Instructions for Completing the Questionnaire

1. This survey is concerned with the salaries of professional positions only. Since the criteria for determining professional status vary among libraries, there is no attempt to define the term "professional." Each library should report the salaries of those staff members it considers professionals, irrespective of membership in a collective bargaining unit, and including, when appropriate, staff who are not librarians in the strict sense of the term, such as systems analysts, budget officers, etc.

2. Salaries should be reported for all filled positions. Vacant positions should be excluded from your report.

3. Report 2005-06 salaries *as they exist on July 1, 2005*. If the library normally increases salaries at a date after July 1, and the salary as of that later date is known or can be estimated (within $100 or so) by the time the questionnaire is due to be returned, please use the higher salary and footnote the effective date and/or whether the reported figures are known or estimated. Please do not hold up the reporting process for later salary adjustments.

4. The Median Salary is the salary that has an equal number of salaries above it and below it. In those libraries with an even number of positions, the median salary is the average of the two salaries that have an equal number of salaries above and below them.

5. The Beginning Professional Salary is the salary that would be paid to a professional without experience, not necessarily the lowest professional salary paid. In reporting the beginning salary, please use a figure that is actually used or likely to be used for entry-level librarians hired by your library.

6. Salaries should be reported for both full-time and part-time professional positions. However, salaries for part-time positions should be converted to their full-time equivalents before reporting; do not report the actual part-time salary paid.

7. Salaries should normally be reported on a 12-month basis. If an appointment is for 9 or 10 months at the option of the employee, the actual salary paid should be increased to its 12-month equivalent. However, if appointments of less than 12 months are required by the employer, report the actual salary paid.

8. The salaries for all professional positions should be included, regardless of whether the salaries come from regular library budget funds or from special funds such as research grants.

9. The salary figures should be straight gross salary figures. Do not include fringe benefits.

10. Explanatory footnotes to the reported figures may be provided when necessary. Footnotes will be included in the published survey.

11. Provide the name of the reporting library and the name of the person who prepares the report.

12. Please return the questionnaire to the ARL Statistics and Measurement Program Office by **September 30, 2005.**

ARL ANNUAL SALARY SURVEY 2005-06
NONUNIVERSITY LIBRARY QUESTIONNAIRE

Part I: Summary Data

Reporting Institution _____ Date Returned to ARL _____

Report Prepared by (name) _____

Title _____

Email address _____ Phone number _____

Contact person (if different) _____

Title _____

Email address _____ Phone number _____

1. Complete the table on the back of this sheet by indicating the number of filled or temporarily vacant professional   positions in each salary range for fiscal years 2004-05 and 2005-06.

2. Median professional salary for fiscal year 2005-06:
    _____

3. Beginning professional salary for 2005-06:
    _____

4. Footnotes (please compare with footnotes from surveys of previous years)

    a. Law Library salaries are included.

        _____ Yes   _____ No   _____ We do not have a Law Library.

    b. Medical Library salaries are included.

        _____ Yes   _____ No   _____ We do not have a Medical Library.

    c. Branch libraries not included (please attach an additional sheet if necessary):

        _____

        _____

5. Other comments (please attach an additional sheet if necessary):

    _____

    _____

Indicate the number of filled professional positions
in each salary range for fiscal years 2004-05 and 2005-06.

| | Number of Positions | |
Salary Range	2004-05	2005-06
More than 250,000		
200,000 - 250,000		
175,000 - 199,999		
150,000 - 174,999		
140,000 - 149,999		
130,000 - 139,999		
120,000 - 129,999		
110,000 - 119,999		
100,000 - 109,999		
95,000 - 99,999		
90,000 - 94,999		
85,000 - 89,999		
80,000 - 84,999		
76,000 - 79,999		
74,000 - 75,999		
72,000 - 73,999		
70,000 - 71,999		
68,000 - 69,999		
66,000 - 67,999		
64,000 - 65,999		
62,000 - 63,999		
60,000 - 61,999		
58,000 - 59,999		
56,000 - 57,999		
54,000 - 55,999		
52,000 - 53,999		
50,000 - 51,999		
48,000 - 49,999		
46,000 - 47,999		
44,000 - 45,999		
42,000 - 43,999		
40,000 - 41,999		
38,000 - 39,999		
36,000 - 37,999		
34,000 - 35,999		
32,000 - 33,999		
30,000 - 31,999		
less than 30,000		

Total Number of Positions

Please return the completed questionnaire to the
ARL Statistics and Measurement Program by **September 30, 2005.**
For assistance, contact Martha Kyrillidou (martha@arl.org), Mark Young (stats-ra@arl.org), or call (202) 296-2296.

FOOTNOTES TO THE ARL ANNUAL SALARY SURVEY, 2005-06

INSTITUTION	NOTE
ALABAMA	Includes Angelo Brund (Business), McClure (Education), Amelia Gayle Gorgas (main), W.S. Hoole (Special Collections), and Rodgers (Science and Engineering) libraries.
ALBERTA	Includes Bibliographic Services, H.T. Coutts Education Library, Humanities and Social Services Library, Faculte Saint-Jean Library, Winspear Business Reference Room, the Office of Staff Development and Training, and Cameron Library (which includes Interlibrary Loans, Financial Systems and Analysis, Science and Technology Library, and Information Technology Services).
ARIZONA STATE	Includes ASU East, ASU West, Hayden, Noble, Music, and Architectural & Environmental Design Libraries.
AUBURN	Includes all Auburn University Libraries, including two branch libraries on the main campus.
BOSTON COLLEGE	Includes O'Neill Library, Bapst Art Library, Burns Library of Rare Books, School of Social Work Library, and the Education Resource Center.
BRIGHAM YOUNG	Excludes BYU-Idaho, BYU-Hawaii, the LDS Business College, and the Salt Lake Center.
BRITISH COLUMBIA	Includes Asian, David Lam (Management), Education, Fine Arts, Koerner, Law, Life Sciences (including Biomedical Branch, Hamber, St. Paul's Hospital, and Woodward Biomedical), MacMillan, Main, Mathematics, Music, and Robson Square libraries, as well as the First Nations House of Learning (Xwi7xwa), the Library Processing Centre, the Rare Books and Special Collections Division, and the Science and Engineering Division.
BROWN	Includes the John Carter Brown Library.
CALIFORNIA, BERKELEY	Includes the General Libraries: Doe, Moffitt, Bancroft, Anthropology, Art History/Classics, Astronomy-Mathematics-Statistics, Bioscience and Natural Resources, Business and Economics, Chemistry, East Asian (including the Center for Chinese Studies), Earth Sciences, Education-Psychology, Engineering, Environmental Design, Music, Optometry, Physics, Public Health (including Health Sciences Information Services, and Occupational and Environmental Health), Social Welfare Libraries, and the Northern Regional Library Facility. Excludes the Affiliated Libraries: Architectural Slide, Continuing Education of the Bar, Earthquake Engineering, Ethnic Studies, Giannini, Institute of Governmental Studies, Institute of Industrial Relations, Institute of International Studies, Institute of Transportation Studies, and Water Resources Center. Also excludes various departmental libraries, e.g., French, History, Philosophy, Rhetoric, and Slavic Languages and Literature.
CALIFORNIA, DAVIS	Includes the Peter J. Shields library, the Physical Sciences and Engineering library, the Carlson Health Sciences Library, and the Agricultural and Resource Economic Library on the Davis campus, as well as the Medical Center Library on the Sacramento campus. Librarians reported as department heads have received administrative stipends that were not included prior to the 2004-05 survey.
CALIFORNIA, LOS ANGELES	Includes the Arts Library, College Library (Undergraduate Library), Eugene and Maxine Rosenfeld Management Library, Music Library, Richard C. Rudolph East Asian Library, Science & Engineering Library, Social Sciences and Humanities Library (Charles E. Young Research Library), and the Southern Regional Library Facility. Also includes data for 11 affiliated libraries on the

INSTITUTION	NOTE
	UCLA campus including the American Indian Studies Center, African American Studies Center, Asian American Studies Center, Chicano Studies Research Center, Ethnomusicology Archive, Film & Television Archive, Graduate School of Education & Information Studies, Institute for Social Science Research, Latin American Center, Olive View Medical Center, and William Andrews Clark Memorial Library.

Louise M. Darling Biomedical Library includes information for the Pacific Southwest Regional Medical Library, an NLM-funded program that is part of the National Network/Libraries of Medicine based in the Biomedical Library.

Librarians reported as department heads have received administrative stipends that were not included prior to the 2004-05 survey. |
| **CALIFORNIA, RIVERSIDE** | Includes Rivera Library (serving the College of Humanities, Arts, and Social Sciences, the School of Education, and the Graduate School of Management), the Science Library (serving the College of Natural and Agricultural Sciences and the College of Engineering), and the Palm Desert Campus Library (serving the Graduate School of Management and the Graduate Division).

Excludes the Media and Music libraries, which have no librarian employees. |
CALIFORNIA, SAN DIEGO	Includes Special Collections, Social Sciences & Humanities, Arts, Science and Engineering, and International Relations & Pacific Studies libraries, as well as the Scripps Institution of Oceanography, the Center for Magnetic Recording and Research, and the Center for Library Instruction and Computing Services.
CALIFORNIA, SANTA BARBARA	Includes Main and Arts Libraries.
CANADA INSTITUTE FOR SCIENTIFIC AND TECHNICAL INFORMATION	Includes all branch libraries.
CHICAGO	Includes all libraries: Science, Medicine, and Law.
COLORADO	Includes Norlin, Music, Business, Math/Physics, Engineering, and Earth Sciences libraries.
COLORADO STATE	Includes Main Campus, Atmospheric Sciences, and Veterinary Medicine libraries.
CONNECTICUT	Includes Avery Point, Greater Hartford, Stamford, Torrington, Waterbury, Archives and Special Collections, Culpeper Media Library, Art and Design, Maps, Music, and Pharmacy libraries.
CORNELL	Includes Africana, Engineering, Entomology, Fine Arts, Geneva Experiment Station, Hotel Administration, Management, Mann, Math, Music, ILR, Olin/Kroch/Uris, Physical Sciences, and Veterinary Medicine libraries.
DARTMOUTH	Includes Music, Sciences, Engineering, Business, Arts and Sciences, and Art libraries.
DUKE	Includes Perkins/Bostock, Chemistry, Biology and Environmental Sciences, Vesic, Marine, Rare Book, and Manuscript and Special Collections libraries.
EMORY	All salaries are effective September 1, 2005 and include the General, Theology, and Oxford College Undergraduate libraries.
FLORIDA	Includes Architecture and Fine Arts, Education, Allen H. Neuharth Journalism and Communications, Judaica, Library West, Marston Science, Music, and Smathers libraries.

Excludes the Legal Information Center. |

INSTITUTION	NOTE
FLORIDA STATE	Includes Strozier, Dirac (Science), Allen (Music), Goldstein, and Career Center libraries, as well as the Panama City ARC and the Ringling Museum in Sarasota.
	Excludes the Panama branch library.
GEORGE WASHINGTON	Includes Gelman, Eckles, and Virginia campus libraries.
GEORGETOWN	Includes the Blommer Science Library (which is a part of the Main Library), the Woodstock Theological Library and the Bioethics Library.
	All libraries have different ranking structures, and the Main Library has eliminated its ranking structure.
GEORGIA	Includes Main, Science, and Student Learning Center libraries, as well as several reading rooms and experiment station libraries around the state.
GEORGIA TECH	Includes Main and Architecture libraries.
GUELPH	Includes the Main campus libraries (McLaughlin Library and the OVC Learning Commons) and the Guelph Humber Learning Commons branch campus library.
	Individual rank data is included for professional librarians only.
HARVARD	Includes all libraries on the Boston and Cambridge campuses, including the Schlesinger Library at Radcliffe College.
	Excludes Biblioteca Berenson in Florence, Italy, and Center for Hellenic Studies and Dumbarton Oaks libraries in Washington, D.C.
HAWAII	Includes Hamilton Library and Sinclair Library.
ILLINOIS, CHICAGO	All salaries are effective September 1, 2005 and include Peoria, Rockford, and Urbana locations.
ILLINOIS, URBANA	Includes all main campus libraries.
INDIANA	Excludes the Indianapolis School of Law, Dentistry, and Medicine Library; IUPUI University Library; Herron School of Art Library; Columbus Library; and Science and Engineering Library, as well as branch campuses at IU-East, IU-Kokomo, IU-Northwest, IU-Southeast, IU-South Bend, and IUPUI-Fort Wayne.
IOWA	Includes the Main library and 10 branch libraries.
IOWA STATE	Includes the Parks (Main) Library and the Veterinary Medical Library.
JOHNS HOPKINS	Includes the Sheridan Libraries, the Friedheim Library, and the School of Advanced International Studies Library.
	Beginning Professional Salary for 2004-05 revised to $42,476.
KENTUCKY	Includes William T. Young Library, the Agricultural Information Center, Architecture Library, Fine Arts Library, Chemistry/Physics Library, Education Library, Engineering Library, Equine Information Center, Geological Sciences Library and Map Collections, International Documents and Research Collections, Kentucky Transportation Center, Lexmark Information Center, Mathematical Sciences Library, and Special Collections & Archives.
KANSAS	Main library includes the Lawrence and Edwards campuses. Medical library

INSTITUTION	NOTE
	includes the Dykes Library.
	Excludes the University of Kansas School of Medicine Library in Wichita, KS, and the Clendening History of Medicine Library in Kansas City, KS.
KENT STATE	Includes the Main Library, the branch libraries (Chemistry/Physics, Architecture, Fashion, Music, Map), and regional libraries (East Liverpool, Ashtabula, Beauga, Trumbul, Tuscarawas, Salem, Stark).
LAVAL	Salaries reported are based on the June 1, 2003 contract, which is still being negotiated.
LIBRARY OF CONGRESS	Salaries include Professional and Administrative positions.
LOUISIANA STATE	Includes the School of Veterinary Medicine.
LOUISVILLE	Includes Ekstrom (Main), Art, Kersey, and Music libraries.
McGILL	Includes the Library Systems Office, Library Technical Services, ILL/Document Delivery, and the Humanities and Social Sciences, Physical Sciences and Engineering, Rare Books, Arts and Architecture, Biology, Education, Management, Islamic Studies, MacDonald, Campus, Music, EDRS, and Government libraries.
	Medical Library data includes the Life Sciences Library and the Osler History of Medicine Library.
McMASTER	Includes Mills Memorial Library, Thode Library of Science and Engineering, Innis (Business) Library, and Health Sciences (which includes Library Services in Northern Ontario).
MANITOBA	Includes Elizabeth Dafoe, Albert D. Cohen, Sciences and Technology, Architecture/Fine Arts/Music, William R. Newman (Agriculture), D.S. Woods (Education), St. John's College, and Fr. Harold Drake libraries.
	Excludes Carolyn Sifton-Helene Fuld St. Boniface Hospital, Victoria General Hospital, Seven Oaks General Hospital, Grace General Hospital, and Concordia Hospital libraries.
MARYLAND	Includes Main library and all branch libraries.
MASSACHUSETTS	Includes DuBois Library (Main), and the Integrated Sciences & Engineering Library.
MIAMI	The General Library data includes 3 non-librarian professional positions, and 2 positions from the Marine branch library.
MICHIGAN	Includes Askwith Media, Asia, Biological Station, Dentistry, Fine Arts, Hatcher Graduate, Map, Art/Architecture/Engineering, Museums, Music , Science, UGL, Social Work, and Special Collections libraries.
	Excludes Bentley, Clements, Kresge Business Administration, and Gerald R. Ford Presidential libraries.
MISSOURI	Includes Main, Journalism, Newspaper, Math, Geology, and Veterinary Medicine libraries.
MONTREAL	Includes Environmental Development, Library and Information Sciences, Botany, Chemistry, Educational Resources, Education-Communication-Psychology-Psychoeducation-Biology, Geography, Kinesiology, Humanities and Social Sciences, Rare Books and Special Collections, Mathematics and Computer Sciences, Veterinary, Music, Optometry, Paramedics, Physics, École

INSTITUTION	NOTE
	Polytechnique, and HEC Montréal libraries.
NATIONAL AGRICULTURAL LIBRARY	All salaries are tracked with benefits.
NEBRASKA	Includes all libraries on the Lincoln campus: Love, Architecture, Engineering, Geology, Mathematics, Music, and C.Y. Thompson.
NEW YORK	Includes Elmer Holmes Bobst, Institute of Fine Arts, Courant, and Real Estate libraries.
NORTH CAROLINA STATE	Includes D.H. Hill (Main), Veterinary Medical, Design, Learning Resources, Natural Resources, and Textiles libraries.
NORTHWESTERN	Includes Main, Science and Engineering, and Schaffner libraries.
NOTRE DAME	Includes the Main and branch campus libraries: Hesburgh, Chemistry/Physics, Kellogg/Kroc Information Center, Architecture, Art Slide, Business Information Center, Life Sciences, Mathematics, and Engineering.
OHIO STATE	Includes Main campus libraries, regional campus libraries, and libraries of the Agricultural Technical Institute and the Ohio Agricultural Research and Development Center.
	Excludes several specialized departmental research libraries on the main campus which are not part of the University Libraries system.
OKLAHOME STATE	Includes Stillwater, Oklahoma City, Okmulgee, Tulsa, and Health Sciences Center libraries.
OREGON	Includes Knight (main), Science, and Architecture & Allied Arts libraries.
PENNSYLVANIA	Includes Main, Business, Music, Fine Arts, Chemistry, Math/Physics/Astronomy, Museum, and Engineering libraries.
PENN STATE	Health Sciences data includes Main, Dental, and Veterinary School libraries. Includes main campus and branches at Abington College, Altoona College, Beaver, Behrend College, Berks-Lehigh Valley College, Capital College, Delaware County, DuBois, Fayette, Penn State Great Valley, Hazelton, Lehigh Valley, McKeesport, Mont Alto, New Kensington, Schuylkill, Shenango, Wilkes-Barre, Worthington, Scranton, and York.
PITTSBURGH	Includes the University Library System.
	Excludes branch campuses at Titusville, Johnstown, Bradford, and Greensburg.
PRINCETON	Includes Main, East Asian, Marquand Art & Archeology, Mudd Library/Archives, Music, Architecture, Astrophysics, Chemistry, Engineering, Fine Hall, Geosciences, Plasma Physics, and Psychology libraries.
PURDUE	All salaries are effective August 15, 2005, in order to reflect a significant restructuring of administrative positions.
	Includes the library system on the West Lafayette campus, consisting of 13 subject libraries and an undergraduate library.
	Excludes the libraries at regional campuses: Purdue North Central (Westville), Purdue Calumet (Hammond), and Indiana University-Purdue University, Fort Wayne.
QUEEN'S	Include Stauffer (humanities & social sciences), Douglas (engineering & science), W.D. Jordan (special collections/music), and Education libraries, as well as the Central Technical Services Unit.

INSTITUTION	NOTE
ROCHESTER	Includes River Campus libraries, Edward G. Miner Medical Library, and Sibley Music Library.
RUTGERS	Includes New Brunswick libraries (Alexander, Mabel Smith Douglass, Kilmer, the Library of Science and Medicine, and its branches), John Cotton Dana Library, Paul Robeson Library, and Technical and Automated Services. Excludes the School of Management and Labor Relations and the Center for Alcohol Studies.
SASKATCHEWAN	Number of employees reported is effective July 1, 2005.
SOUTH CAROLINA	Includes the Thomas Cooper (Main) Library.
SOUTHERN CALIFORNIA	Main Libraries include: Accounting, Applied Social Sciences, Architecture and Fine Arts, Business, Cinema-Television, East Asian, Gerontology, Grand Ave. and Book Depository, Leavey (College), Music, Science and Engineering, Specialized Libraries and Archival Collections.
SUNY-BUFFALO	Includes Arts and Sciences Libraries, Music Library, and Special Collections (Archives, Poetry, and Rare Books).
SYRACUSE	Includes the Main campus library, the Science and Technology Library, the Geology Library. The Math Library and the Physics Library.
TEXAS	Includes Center for American History, Harry Ransom Humanities Research Center, and the University of Texas Libraries.
TEXAS A&M	All salaries are effective September 1, 2005 and include Main, Policy Services & Economics, and Business libraries. Excludes the Medical Sciences Library and the Texas A&M Library at Galveston.
TEXAS TECH	All salaries are effective September 1, 2005 and include the University Library, Southwest Collection/Special Collections Library, Architecture Library, International Cultural Center Library, Geosciences Library, and Vietnam Archives Library.
TORONTO	Includes Robarts, Engineering and Computer Science, Dentistry, Chemistry, School of Management, Physics, Faculty of Information Services, Media Commons, Astronomy, Rare Book, Criminology, Music, St. Michael's College, New College, Earth Sciences, and East Asian libraries, as well as the Ontario Institute for Studies in Education, the University of Toronto-Scarborough, the University of Toronto-Mississauga, and the Centre for Industrial Relations. Medical Library includes the Gerstein Science and Information Centre and the Family and Community Medicine Library.
TULANE	Due to damage from Hurricane Katrina, Tulane was unable to submit salary data for 2005-06. Instead, a 3% increase was applied to the institution-wide data from 2004-05, and the same Beginning Professional Salary was used again.
VANDERBILT	Includes Central, Divinity, Peabody, Management, and Science and Engineering libraries, as well as the Special Collections/University Archives, Centralized Technical Services, Library Information Services, Administration, and TV News Archive. Excludes 13 non-librarian exempt positions from the Library that were included in past years.

INSTITUTION	NOTE
VIRGINIA	Includes Alderman (main), Clemons (undergraduate), Education, Fiske Kimball Fine Arts, Music, Science/Engineering (6 libraries), Small Special Collections, and Darden Graduate Business libraries.
	Excludes the University of Virginia College at Wise.
WASHINGTON	Includes the University Libraries on the Seattle campus.
	Excludes the campus libraries at the University of Washington-Bothell and University of Washington-Tacoma.
WASHINGTON STATE	All salaries are effective September 1, 2005 to reduce salary compression issues, and include WSU-Pullman, WSU-spokane, WSU-ICN, the Energy Library, WSU-Tri-Cities, and WSU-Vancouver.
WASINGTON U. – St. LOUIS	Includes Central Library and departmental libraries in Biology, Business, Chemistry, Art & Architecture, Earth Sciences, East Asian, Math, Music, Physics, and Social Work.
WATERLOO	Includes Dana Porter Library, Davis Centre Library, University Map Library, and Musagetes Library.
WESTERN ONTARIO	Includes D.B. Weldon, Business, Education, Music, and Allyn and Betty Taylor libraries.
	Excludes the Affiliated College libraries: King's University College, Huron University College, and Brescia University College.
	No rank structure was reported for 2005-06, due to ongoing negotiations between Librarians and Archivists.
WISCONSIN	Includes Memorial, College, Art, Biology, Business, Chemistry, Geography, Geology and Geophysics, Mathematics, Music, Physics, Social Science Reference, Social Work, Steenbock Agricultural and Life Sciences, and Wendt Engineering libraries.
	Excludes the CIMC (School of Education), ShIS, Map, and Primate libraries.
YORK	All salaries are effective September 1, 2005 and include Scott, Map, Sound & Moving Image, Steacie Science and Engineering, Peter F. Bronfman Business, Leslie Frost, and Osgoode Hall Law libraries, as well as Archives and Special Collections.

APPENDICES

APPENDIX A
ARL Member Libraries as of January 1, 2006

The Association of Research Libraries (ARL) represents the interests of 124 libraries that serve major North American research institutions. The ARL Statistics and Measurement program is organized around identifying, collecting, analyzing, and distributing quantifiable information describing the characteristics of research libraries.

Institution	Category	Full Name of Institution	Location
Alabama	S	University of Alabama	Tuscaloosa, Alabama
Alberta	C	University of Alberta	Edmonton, Alberta
Arizona	S	University of Arizona	Tucson, Arizona
Arizona State	S	Arizona State University	Tempe, Arizona
Auburn	S	Auburn University	Auburn, Alabama
Boston	P	Boston University	Boston, Massachusetts
Boston College	P	Boston College	Boston, Massachusetts
Brigham Young	P	Brigham Young University	Provo, Utah
British Columbia	C	University of British Columbia	Vancouver, British Columbia
Brown	P	Brown University	Providence, Rhode Island
Berkeley, California	S	University of California, Berkeley	California, Berkeley
California, Davis	S	University of California, Davis	Davis, California
California, Irvine	S	University of California, Irvine	Irvine, California
California, Los Angeles	S	University of California, Los Angeles	Los Angeles, California
California, Riverside	S	University of California, Riverside	Riverside, California
California, San Diego	S	University of California, San Diego	La Jolla, California
California, Santa Barbara	S	University of California, Santa Barbara	Santa Barbara, California
Case Western Reserve	P	Case Western Reserve University	Cleveland, Ohio
Chicago	P	University of Chicago	Chicago, Illinois
Cincinnati	S	University of Cincinnati	Cincinnati, Ohio
Colorado	S	University of Colorado	Boulder, Colorado
Colorado State	S	Colorado State University	Fort Collins, Colorado
Columbia	P	Columbia University	New York, New York
Connecticut	S	University of Connecticut	Storrs, Connecticut
Cornell	P	Cornell University	Ithaca, New York
Dartmouth	P	Dartmouth College	Hanover, New Hampshire
Delaware	S	University of Delaware	Newark, Delaware
Duke	P	Duke University	Durham, North Carolina
Emory	P	Emory University	Atlanta, Georgia
Florida	S	University of Florida	Gainesville, Florida
Flordia State	S	Florida State University	Tallahassee, Florida
George Washington	P	George Washington University	Washington, D.C.
Georgetown	P	Georgetown University	Washington, D.C.
Georgia	S	University of Georgia	Athens, Georgia
Georgia Tech	S	Georgia Institute of Technology	Atlanta, Georgia
Guelph	C	University of Guelph	Guelph, Ontario
Harvard	P	Harvard University	Cambridge, Massachusetts
Hawaii	S	University of Hawaii	Honolulu, Hawaii
Houston	S	University of Houston	Houston, Texas
Howard	P	Howard University	Washington, D.C.
Illinois, Chicago	S	University of Illinois at Chicago	Chicago, Illinois
Illinois, Urbana	S	University of Illinois at Urbana	Urbana, Illinois
Indiana	S	Indiana University	Bloomington, Indiana
Iowa	S	University of Iowa	Iowa City, Iowa
Iowa State	S	Iowa State University	Ames, Iowa
Johns Hopkins	P	Johns Hopkins University	Baltimore, Maryland
Kansas	S	University of Kansas	Lawrence, Kansas
Kent State	S	Kent State University	Kent, Ohio
Kentucky	S	University of Kentucky	Lexington, Kentucky
Laval	C	Laval University	Quebec, Quebec
Louisiana State	S	Louisiana State University	Baton Rouge, Louisiana
Louisville	S	University of Louisville	Louisville, Kentucky
McGill	C	McGill University	Montreal, Quebec
McMaster	C	McMaster University	Hamilton, Ontario
Manitoba	C	University of Manitoba	Winnipeg, Manitoba
Maryland	S	University of Maryland	College Park, Maryland
Massachusetts	S	University of Massachusetts	Amherst, Massachusetts
MIT	P	Massachusetts Institute of Technology	Cambridge, Massachusetts

S=U.S. public university   P=U.S. private university   N=U.S. nonuniversity library   C=Canadian university   X=Canadian nonuniversity

Institution	Category	Full Name of Institution	Location
Miami	P	University of Miami	Coral Gables, Florida
Michigan	S	University of Michigan	Ann Arbor, Michigan
Michigan State	S	Michigan State University	East Lansing, Michigan
Minnesota	S	University of Minnesota	Minneapolis, Minnesota
Missouri	S	University of Missouri	Columbia, Missouri
Montreal	C	University of Montreal	Montreal, Quebec
Nebraska	S	University of Nebraska-Lincoln	Lincoln, Nebraska
New Mexico	S	University of New Mexico	Albuquerque, New Mexico
New York	P	New York University	New York, New York
North Carolina	S	University of North Carolina	Chapel Hill, North Carolina
North Carolina State	S	North Carolina State University	Raleigh, North Carolina
Northwestern	P	Northwestern University	Evanston, Illinois
Notre Dame	P	University of Notre Dame	Notre Dame, Indiana
Ohio	S	Ohio University	Athens, Ohio
Ohio State	S	Ohio State University	Columbus, Ohio
Oklahoma	S	University of Oklahoma	Norman, Oklahoma
Oklahoma State	S	Oklahoma State University	Stillwater, Oklahoma
Oregon	S	University of Oregon	Eugene, Oregon
Pennsylvania	P	University of Pennsylvania	Philadelphia, Pennsylvania
Pennsylvania State	S	Pennsylvania State University	University Park, Pennsylvania
Pittsburgh	S	University of Pittsburgh	Pittsburgh, Pennsylvania
Princeton	P	Princeton University	Princeton, New Jersey
Purdue	S	Purdue University	West Lafayette, Indiana
Queen's	C	Queen's University	Kingston, Ontario
Rice	P	Rice University	Houston, Texas
Rochester	P	University of Rochester	Rochester, New York
Rutgers	S	Rutgers University	New Brunswick, New Jersey
Saskatchewan	C	University of Saskatchewan	Saskatoon, Saskatchewan
South Carolina	S	University of South Carolina	Columbia, South Carolina
Southern California	P	University of Southern California	Los Angeles, California
Southern Illinois	S	Southern Illinois University	Carbondale, Illinois
SUNY-Albany	S	University at Albany, State University of New York	Albany, New York
SUNY-Buffalo	S	University at Buffalo, State University of New York	Buffalo, New York
SUNY-Stony Brook	S	State University of New York at Stony Brook	Stony Brook, New York
Syracuse	P	Syracuse University	Syracuse, New York
Temple	S	Temple University	Philadelphia, Pennsylvania
Tennessee	S	University of Tennessee	Knoxville, Tennessee
Texas	S	University of Texas	Austin, Texas
Texas A&M	S	Texas A&M University	College Station, Texas
Texas Tech	S	Texas Tech University	Lubbock, Texas
Toronto	C	University of Toronto	Toronto, Ontario
Tulane	P	Tulane University	New Orleans, Louisiana
Utah	S	University of Utah	Salt Lake City, Utah
Vanderbilt	P	Vanderbilt University	Nashville, Tennessee
Virginia	S	University of Virginia	Charlottesville, Virginia
Virginia Tech	S	Virginia Polytechnic Institute & State University	Blacksburg, Virginia
Washington	S	University of Washington	Seattle, Washington
Washington State	S	Washington State University	Pullman, Washington
Washington U.-St. Louis	P	Washington University	St. Louis, Missouri
Waterloo	C	University of Waterloo	Waterloo, Ontario
Wayne State	S	Wayne State University	Detroit, Michigan
Western Ontario	C	University of Western Ontario	London, Ontario
Wisconsin	S	University of Wisconsin	Madison, Wisconsin
Yale	P	Yale University	New Haven, Connecticut
York	C	York University	North York, Ontario
Boston Public Library	N	Boston Public Library	Boston, Massachusetts
Canada Inst. SciTech Info.	X	Canada Inst. for Scientific & Technical Information	Ottawa, Ontario
Center for Research Libs.	N	Center for Research Libraries	Chicago, Illinois
Library of Congress	N	Library of Congress	Washington, D.C.
Natl. Agricultural Lib.	N	National Agricultural Library	Beltsville, Maryland
Library & Archives of Canada	X	Library and Archives of Canada*	Ottawa, Ontario
Natl. Library of Medicine	N	National Library of Medicine	Bethesda, Maryland
New York Public Library	N	New York Public Library	New York, New York
New York State Library	N	New York State Library	Albany, New York
Smithsonian Institution	N	Smithsonian Institution	Washington, D.C.

S=U.S. public university   P=U.S. private university   N=U.S. nonuniversity library   C=Canadian university   X=Canadian nonuniversity

APPENDIX B
TABLE NUMBERING CHANGES 1998-99 TO 1999-2000

From 1998-99 to 1999-2000 a number of new tables were added to *ARL Annual Salary Survey* publication and some old tables were renumbered. As a result of these changes, a new section was added, entitled **U.S. ARL University Libraries,** which includes Tables 26 and 29. Two new tables showing averages for all U.S. and Canadian institutions were also included as Table 3 and Table 4. The table below maps the old table-numbering scheme to the new one for purposes of comparison.

Old	New	
		SALARY LEVELS FOR STAFF IN ARL LIBRARIES
1	1	Distribution by Salary Level
12	2	Salary Trends in ARL University Libraries
N/A	3	Salary Trends in U.S. ARL University Libraries
N/A	4	Salary Trends in Canadian ARL University Libraries
		ARL NONUNIVERSITY LIBRARIES
2	5	Median and Beginning Professional Salaries in ARL Nonuniversity Libraries
3	6	Salary Trends in ARL Nonuniversity Libraries
		ARL UNIVERSITY LIBRARIES
4	7	Filled Positions; Average, Median, Beginning Professional Salaries; And Average Years of Professional Experience in ARL University Libraries, FY 1999-2000
5	8	Beginning Professional Salaries in ARL University Libraries; Rank Order Table, FY 1998-99
6	9	Beginning Professional Salaries in ARL University Libraries; Rank Order Table, FY 1999-2000
7	10	Median Professional Salaries in ARL University Libraries; Rank Order Table, FY 1998-99
8	11	Median Professional Salaries in ARL University Libraries; Rank Order Table, FY 1999-2000
9	12	Average Professional Salaries in ARL University Libraries; Rank Order Table, FY 1998-99
10	13	Average Professional Salaries in ARL University Libraries; Rank Order Table, FY 1999-2000
11	14	Average, Median, and Beginning Professional Salaries in ARL UniversityLibraries; Summary of Rankings, FYs 1996-97 to 1999-2000
13	15	Distribution of Professional Staff in ARL University Libraries by Salary and Position, FY 1999-2000
14	16	Distribution of Professional Staff in ARL University Libraries by Salary, Sex, and Position, FY 1999-2000
15	17	Number and Average Salaries of ARL University Librarians by Position and Sex, FY 1999-2000
17	18	Number and Average Years of Experience of ARL University Librarians by Position and Sex, FY 1999-2000
19	19	Number and Average Salaries of ARL University Librarians by Years of Experience and Sex, FY 1999-2000
21	20	Average Salaries of ARL University Librarians by Years of Experience, FY 1999-2000
22	21	Number and Average Salaries of ARL University Librarians by Position and Type of Institution, FY 1999-2000
22b	22	Years of Experience of ARL University Librarians by Position and Type of Institution, FY 1999-2000
23	23	Number and Average Salaries of ARL University Librarians by Position and Size of Professional Staff, FY 1999-2000
23b	24	Years of Experience of ARL University Librarians by Position and Size of Professional Staff, FY 1999-2000
24	25	Average Salaries of ARL University Librarians by Position and Geographic Region, FY 1999-2000

ARL Statistics and Measurement Program
PUBLICATIONS AND SERVICES
http://www.arl.org/

ARL Academic Law Library Statistics
ISSN 1538-8999 • Back issues are available • Standing order offered
> Yearly report of data for collections' size and growth, materials and operating expenditures, staffing, and public service activities in ARL university law libraries. Includes comparisons to the larger research collections at each university.

ARL Academic Medical Library Statistics
ISSN 1538-9006 • Back issues are available • Standing order offered
> Yearly report of data for collections' size and growth, materials and operating expenditures, staffing, and public service activities in ARL university medical libraries. Includes comparisons to the larger research collections at each university.

ARL Preservation Statistics
ISSN 1050-7442 • Back issues are available • Standing order offered
> Annual compilation of data on current levels of preservation efforts and reports on the key organizational, functional, and fiscal components comprising ARL preservation programs.

ARL Statistics
ISSN 0147-2135 • Back issues are available • Standing order offered
> Annual compilation of data on collection size and growth, materials and operating expenditures, staffing, and library services. The most comprehensive resource for information on research library operations and trends.

User Surveys in Academic Libraries
> This workshop presents the basic concepts and steps for conducting a user survey: defining objectives, sampling, measurement scales, logistics, data analysis, and report writing.

Electronic Publishing of Data Sets on the World Wide Web
> This three-day workshop is designed for librarians, information professionals, and educators. It provides hands-on experience in developing interfaces for publishing and analyzing social, economic, and other numeric data sets on the WWW.

Customized Services
> For any dataset produced by ARL, one can request comparative institutional data and ARL will perform the analysis and provide tables and reports in the format best suited to the need.

For more information on any of these products or services, please contact Martha Kyrillidou, Senior Program Officer for Statistics and Measurement, at 202-296-2296 or email at martha@arl.org.